"...one nation, under God, indivisible, with liberty and justice for all."

Under the shredded banner of this myth, people are still living in rat-infested ghettos, children are deprived of a decent education, minority applicants find jobs hard to get, and violence continually erupts. **RACISM** looks into the origins and development of attitudes which are dividing and destroying our nation. The book discusses questions which are not easily resolved and describes some steps which are being taken in the long, hard battle to combat prejudice. Fifteen selected articles confront the reader with situations to which he cannot fail to respond.

"We will have to repent in this generation not merely for the vitriolic words and actions of the bad people, but for the appalling silence of the good people. We must come to see that human progress never rolls in on the wheels of inevitability. It comes from the tireless efforts and persistent work of men...."

—Martin Luther King, Jr.

**RACISM**
is an original POCKET BOOK edition.

PROBLEMS OF AMERICAN SOCIETY

Focusing on the urban scene, youth, the individual and his search for a better life, the books in this series probe the most crucial dilemmas of our time.

*The Negro in the City*
*Civil Rights and Civil Liberties*
*Crime and Juvenile Delinquency*
*Poverty and the Poor*
*Air and Water Pollution*
*The Traffic Jam*
*The Slums*
*The Draft*
*The City as a Community*
*The Consumer*
*Drugs*
*Riots*
*Minorities All*
*Governing the City*
*Hunger*
*Prisons*
*The Police*
*Racism*

ANITA
MONTE

# RACISM

PUBLISHED BY POCKET BOOKS NEW YORK

**RACISM**

POCKET BOOK edition published March, 1972

Cover photograph courtesy of United Press International, Inc.

This original POCKET BOOK edition is printed from
brand-new plates made from newly set, clear, easy-to-read type.
POCKET BOOK editions are published by POCKET BOOKS, a division of
Simon & Schuster, Inc., 630 Fifth Avenue, New York, N.Y. 10020.
Trademarks registered in the United States and other countries.

L

## ACKNOWLEDGMENT

For their participation in making this book possible, the author and general editor wish to thank the writers and publishers who permitted their articles to be reprinted here. We also thank the photographers and photographic services contributing the visuals reproduced in the book. The pictures on pages 21, 22 and 145 were obtained through the courtesy of Rayna Green, whose Ph.D. thesis (Indiana University, 1971) is an extensive study of the Anglo-American image of the Indian. We are grateful to the Anti-Defamation League of B'nai B'rith for their information and guidance in preparing this book. The work and cooperation of the editorial staff of WASHINGTON SQUARE PRESS on behalf of POCKET BOOKS is greatly appreciated.

# Preface

This is one of a series of volumes intended to become text materials for urban schools as well as for the general reader. For the most part, the issues chosen for the *Problems of American Society* series have been those associated with urban America. The American racial problem is different. It is different because racism has long been a factor in American life. Racism was a factor in American life when this was a rural, not an urban, nation. It has roots deep in European traditions and in the customs, habits, and teachings of ancient society. It has taken many forms and has not always been easy to recognize. Few, if any, groups in American society are free of racial prejudices. Thus, the Populists of several generations ago, while eager to urge the adoption of such liberal and forward-looking measures as government regulation of industry, a graduated income tax, and the direct election of Senators, nevertheless were also deeply hostile to the foreigner, to the immigrant, and to the Jew. As recently as 1960 when John F. Kennedy won the Presidential race, his Catholicism was a factor that was still voiced against him.

That all men are brothers has often been taken as a meaningless cliché mouthed for the occasion that seemed appropriate to the moment, but then was forgotten. In point of fact, all men do have common ancestors and race has no foundation in scientific thought. Yet, at all times and in all places men have capitalized on the prejudices of man to promote their own causes, to further their own ambitions, and to exclude from their company those whose religion, color, or point of origin seemed to be different from their own.

As in other volumes in this series, the subject is introduced by a brief essay in which we have tried to show the dynamics of racial questions. In doing so we have raised more questions than we have answered. Such was our intent. This is but an introductory study and the readings that follow the essay are designed to be introductory readings to the literature in a vast and important field.

It is hard to understand both the long history of racism on the one hand and its continued existence on the other. Men, otherwise intelligent, have often displayed racist feelings. What can be done about it is difficult to say. While the answers may well be found in society and its institutions, the battle against racism to destroy the seeds of prejudice innocently and sometimes not so innocently planted, must be waged within the individual. Perhaps by recognizing that it is there, by trying to do something to overcome it, each of us can help to destroy the seeds before they flower and prevent a reseeding in the innocent souls of those who follow.

G. L.

# Contents

# Contents

# Part One

# The Problem
# and the
# Challenge

With their escort of troopers, two of the nine black students attending Central High School, Little Rock, Arkansas, arrive for classes. (Wide World)

THE HIGH SCHOOL was set back from the street. It was bordered with neatly clipped hedges and an immaculately tailored lawn. The structure was old, but it carried its age with a charm that helped to enhance the picturesque setting which so pleasantly met the eye. An old-model car pulled to the curb, the door opened, and two black children stepped onto the sidewalk. With tense, fearful faces the children began the long, frightening walk up the stairs and down a pathway that led to the entrance of the school. On either side of them a seemingly endless gauntlet of jeering whites hooted and screamed at them along the way. When the doors swung open, a new era was ushered in. For the first time in this school's existence, a black child crossed the threshold in search of an elusive prize which previously had been as distant as the stars: the right to an education equal to that of his white brothers.

This prize was made possible by a decision of the United States Supreme Court in 1954. In the case of *Brown v. Board of Education of Topeka,* the Court, rejecting the "separate but equal" concept for the public schools of the nation, declared "separate educational facilities are inherently unequal."

The attitude toward white racists is shown in this demonstration by blacks. (Joe Molnar)

It is depressing to think that human beings could turn upon one another in a land where there are enough resources for all to live in harmony. But, with pretended unawareness or total indifference, millions of people had witnessed the degradation of an entire group. The inevitable aftermath arrived: the era of confrontation between black and white, an open conflict between fellow Americans.

The violent results of the historic Supreme Court decision cost this country a serious loss of prestige among the nations of the world. To men of justice, the idea that schoolchildren could be abused was appalling, and for millions of citizens everywhere the sickness that is racism struck with full impact for the first time.

## What Is Racism?

Racism is a virulent form of prejudice. Prejudice is the detrimental, preconceived judgment of individuals or groups on the basis of their skin color, culture, speech patterns, mode of dress, or whatever. When we prejudge people, we sometimes react with feelings of hatred, fear, and suspicion.

Racism leads to discrimination. When we discriminate, we exclude certain groups. When we perceive a difference in others, we compare them to ourselves or our group and irrationally decide that they are inferior because they are different from us—and therefore should not share our society or privileges.

## What Is Race?

Do we know what we mean when we use the word *race?* Scientists qualified in the study of mankind say we do not.

"Confusing words make for confusing thought. In turn confused thinking makes for confused behavior, and confused behavior can be very dangerous. Therefore, we must be careful in the use of our words. The word 'ethnic' is derived from the Greek word *ethnos,* which originally meant a tribe, people, nation, or a group. The term 'ethnic group' is a good one to use instead of 'race' for the following reasons: 1) The person using it is likely to know what he is talking about, whereas the person who uses the term 'race' is not; 2) It raises a question rather than makes the assumption that everyone understands what is meant by the term 'race.' The person who hears the term 'ethnic group' is likely to ask you what you mean by it, and that at once affords an opportunity for clarification as to the facts and the correction of erroneous actions. The term 'ethnic group' serves as a challenge to thought and as a stimulus to rethink the foundation of one's beliefs. Where the term 'race' closes the door on understanding, the term 'ethnic group' opens it."[1]

Since most scientists agree that we all come from one basic source, whatever our color, type of hair, or physical characteristics, we must assume that there is only one race—the race of mankind. How, then, do scientists account for the physical differences between different groups? "[A]s the population grew some families decided to strike out for themselves."[2] The culmination of many years found groups of mankind scattered throughout the continents, and natural evolvement produced the pigmentation of skin and hair most adaptable to the region in which a group had chosen to live.

This environmental adaptation resulted in what became the scientific adoption of the three anthropological classifications of man: Negroid, Mongoloid, and Caucasoid. Negroid includes many types; they may be black-skinned with kinky hair, or white-skinned with long, straight blond hair, or olive-skinned with thin lips, aquiline nose, and blue eyes, or black with a long narrow nose, brown eyes, and long straight hair, and so on. Caucasoid includes whites and nonwhites, such as the people of India, the Australian aborigines, and the Ainu of Japan. Mongoloid includes the Chinese, Japanese, Malaysians, and other Orientals.

The uninformed speak of the yellow, white, black,

or brown race. As noted, these terms are incorrect. Color classification does not identify groups as races.

Race is also confused with nationality. There is no such thing as the Irish, French, or German races. The people who live in these countries are members of individual nations but may be of many different racial origins.

Another view is that racial characteristics are transmitted from one generation to another and that they determine physical and intellectual traits as well as character and ability. Thus we tend to judge people on the basis of their physical appearance. As an example, if a white reporter entered a large newsroom equally divided between white and nonwhite reporters and had to decide on his own initiative who the managing editor was, he would probably look for a white individual. A basic misinterpretation of race would lead him to assume that, because of supposed racial intellectual superiority, a white man would be in charge. So overpowering has this emotional response become through application over the generations that a nonwhite reporter might react in like manner! (For amplification of this discussion see Reading 1.)

Often efforts have been made to find a superior race. Hitler tried to impose such a theory with his mouthings of Nordic or Aryan supremacy. Again, there is no such thing, and attempts to identify a superior race are expressions of the worst forms of racism.

The term race is also confused with religion. Jews are often referred to as a race. They are not. To be Jewish is to belong to a religious group. Jews may be Negroid, Mongoloid, or Caucasoid, and they resemble the groups of people among whom they live.

They may be members of a particular nation and as such are Russians, Germans, or Americans.

Although it is generally inaccurate to include ethnic and religious prejudice in a study of racism, we do so because racism is an emotional response based on false meanings and confusion. As used in this book, therefore, racism refers to any problems created by one group's efforts to undermine the value of another.

## How Widespread Is Racism?

Racism is not new. The disease is as old as mankind. Long before the Christian Era, the Chaldeans enslaved the Hebrews, who were later enslaved by the Egyptians. Orientals were conquered and enslaved by the Romans.

Racism and other forms of discrimination have caused civil wars and have formed the basis for wars between nations. In the name of race, millions of Jews were murdered in World War II by Hitler, who said to Hermann Rauschning:

> I know perfectly well, just as all those tremendously clever intellectuals, that in the scientific sense there is no such thing as race. And I, as a politician, need a conception which enables the order which has hitherto existed on historic bases to be abolished, and an entirely new and anti-historic order enforced and given an intellectual basis. . . . With the conception of race, National Socialism will carry the revolution abroad and recast the world.[3]

Even the United States government used racist tactics to win a war. In a program of total saturation,

Anti-Japanese propaganda posters used during World War II. (Poster Originals)

Vanguard of more than 100,000 Japanese-Americans assemble to be moved under Army convoy to a center at Owens Valley, near Los Angeles, during World War II. (Herald Tribune)

this country unleashed a propaganda barrage against Japan that likened the Japanese to the vilest animals that stalked the earth. To be Japanese was to be a mutilator of children, a raper of women, and a yellow, squint-eyed, demented creature who lived only to kill. Americans of Japanese descent were interned in camps—on the one hand, to protect them from violence that the government, itself, had encouraged, and on the other hand, because the government feared that Japanese-Americans could not be loyal to the United States under the pressure of war.

Today countries scattered throughout the world embrace racism as a way of life. South Africa has thrived for years on a program of racial subjugation. Jews have been scorned and abused in almost every country in the world. Australia and New Zealand have racist policies; nonwhites are not welcome as immigrants.

How Has Racism Evolved in the United States?

From the very early days of the United States, racism, prejudice, and discrimination have existed in every generation in various forms.

Almost from the time the white settlers set foot upon this continent, they instituted a barbaric approach to a people whom they considered savages. The rich land that belonged to the Indians was slowly gobbled up by the white man's greed until the Indian found himself a prisoner in his own land. The white man cruelly tried to subdue and eventually obliterate the Indian by actual genocide.

A typical portrayal of conflict with Indians. (Library of Congress)

Posters like these were common. (Shelburne Museum, Inc.)

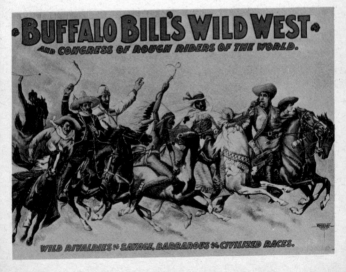

The American Indians as a cultural group were subjected to much more hatred and degradation than the blacks. Both were considered "niggers," one red, one black. But the Indian was free and dangerous and ever ready to fight for what was rightfully his. His aggressiveness was that spark that kept the fire of hate burning.

Many of the so-called reservations later set aside for the Indians by the politicians of the day were barren and barely usable portions of land. Little by little the Indians were reduced to a helpless minority. Even today the plight of the American Indian weighs heavily on the American conscience. (See Reading 2.)

In the Mexican-American War (1846–1848) racism was the justification the white man used in conspiring to acquire lands from the Mexicans in order to form slave states. (Today the Chicanos are fighting in the courts of New Mexico for the restoration of their ancestral land.) With a fervent, righteous belief that any group other than one with white skin was by nature inferior, this nation vindicated the importation of black slaves, and later, Filipinos, Puerto Ricans, and Mexicans as cheap labor.

We have even exported our poison of racism! During World War I our discriminatory practices against black soldiers influenced the publication on August 7, 1918, of *A French Directive* to the French military stationed with the American army:

. . . American opinion is unanimous on the "color question," and does not admit it any discussion.

The increasing number of Negroes in the United States (about 15,000,000) would create for the white race in the Republic a menace of degeneracy were it not that an impassable gulf has been made between them. . . .

Degradation of the Negro slave depicted in cartoon of 1864.
(The New York Public Library Picture Collection)

The French public has been accustomed to treat-
ing the Negro with familiarity and indulgence.

This indulgence and this familiarity . . . are
matters of grievous concern to the Americans.
They consider them an affront to their national
policy. They are afraid that contact with the
French will inspire in black Americans aspirations
which to them (the whites) appear intolerable.

It is of the utmost importance that every effort
be made to avoid profoundly estranging American
opinion.

"Liberty and justice for all."   (Joe Molnar)

Although a citizen of the United States, the black man is regarded by the white American as an inferior being. . . .[4]

Racism, prejudice, and discrimination are as much part of the American legacy as is our theme of brotherhood. Despite our legal and religious declarations of "liberty and justice for all" and "love thy neighbor as thyself," racism has been a part of our social structure in all forms. No one, white or nonwhite, can escape its influences on our society, our thinking, our instincts. In the past, we have been anti-Irish, anti-Italian, anti-Polish, anti-German. Today ethnic hostilities are directed more against blacks, Puerto Ricans, Mexicans, and Indians. We hear of "the dumb Swede," "the drunken Irishman," "the depraved French," "the horse-faced Englishman." The words "kike," "nigger," "wop," "greaser," and others are spouted so easily. Statements like "You can't trust a Jew," "Niggers are shiftless," and "Don't give an Indian whiskey; he'll go crazy," perpetuate prejudicial myths. Hardly anyone is exempt from discriminatory clichés.

Today there even exist prejudicial feeling and discriminatory actions against many white youth because of their clothing and hairstyles. They are denied jobs, living quarters, and entrances to other avenues of society because they dare to be different. They are labeled "troublemakers" and "dropouts" because they dare to dress differently from the mainstream of America. However, once they cut their hair and dress according to the rules of the establishment, avenues that were closed to them are immediately opened.

But a nonwhite youth attired in an antiestablishment manner finds that a mere change of clothing

This black youth asserts his Afro identity. (Fortune Monte)

and a new hairstyle does not free him from racism or discrimination: the color of his skin is the criterion which limits where he can earn a living, socialize, live, and learn.

If racism is acceptable to those we elect to power, then it stands to reason that the man in the street should find it easy to embrace. It weaves and interweaves itself into a pattern that finds its way into almost every social structure.

What is it that enables one man to degrade another? Since we preach "charity for all," why do we remain a nation of bigots? Why is there still a hiatus between principle and practice? This leads us to the questions: Is it possible to enforce legislation effectively against discrimination as long as individuals harbor racist beliefs? Should there be a concerted attempt to change people's attitudes?

Racial hostility runs deep. We are not born racists; we learn to be racists from our parents, friends, teachers—from our educational, religious, political, and social institutions. Yet, there is no way to pass a law eliminating racism, for the right to one's thoughts is beyond the reach of any government. It is only when one's racial thoughts are expressed in acts of discrimination that the government can attempt to eradicate racism. A government can pass laws only about what one does, not about what one believes. But to pass and enforce laws against discrimination without, at the same time, attempting to change the bigot's attitude is delusionary. Since it is almost impossible to change attitudes overnight, bigotry persists.

How Have American Institutions Contributed to Racism?

America was founded on the principle that human rights are universal and the birthright of all men regardless of race, color, or creed. And although this country paid homage to the melting-pot theory by accepting people from all over the world, in practice, certain groups have always been denied their human rights; they were never accepted in significant numbers into the mainstream of white American society.

Every society establishes institutions to perpetuate its values and traditions. In our society the institutions were, and still are, white. They are structured so that the white middle-class culture is the acceptable one. Minority cultures within our "melting pot" are separate identities and they remain separate communities. The dominant American life-style does not include the cultures of the Mexican-American, the Puerto Rican-American, the Indian-American, the black-American, the Oriental-American. (See Reading 3.)

As a result, white America has a false idea of the minority cultures, while these cultural groups have little idea of their own value. Any institution that is advantageous solely to whites and disadvantageous to nonwhites is a racist institution. In what ways, then, have our institutions reflected racial prejudice?

*Education*

In the field of education, segregation of schools by race has been legally mandatory in many states. In others, separate education facilities grew out of patterns of racial discrimination in housing. In 1954, mandatory segregation was declared unconstitutional by the Supreme Court. Yet in 1967, the United States Commission on Civil Rights said: "The majority of American children continue to attend schools that are largely segregated. . . . Racial isolation in the public schools is extensive and has increased since 1954."[5] Almost 20 years later, we are still arguing over ways and means of enforcing the 1954 decision. Some states are using every legal trick to avoid enforcing it altogether.

In most schools, American history is still taught from a white middle-class point of view. From the conflicts with the Indians to the Second World War, minorities are discriminated against in social studies texts. Facts are distorted to present a picture of white superiority. The Indian always massacred the white man. The white man always fought to a gallant victory over the red man. Few texts made any mention of the black man except to say that he was of African descent and was a victim of slavery. In like manner, other minorities have not been given positive treatment in many textbooks.

Consider, as an example, what the effects are on young minds reading *The Merchant of Venice* by Shakespeare, which is required reading in many literature classes. Shylock, a Jew, is portrayed as an evil, inhumane, greedy moneylender whose lust for gold is all-consuming. In contrast, Antonio—a Christian —is shown as the epitome of virtue, charity, love, and goodness. The image of Shylock in literature has become in reality the stereotype of the Jew.

Also read often in school is Dickens's *Oliver Twist* in which Fagin is portrayed as a Jew who taught deserted children to pick pockets and steal for him. For all its charm in other respects, *Oliver Twist* persists in maintaining the stereotype of the Jew as a social outcast. In numerous works of great and not so great literature, the black, too, is portrayed in the caricature of a shiftless, lazy, playful, indolent-but-happy child—no matter what his age. Mark Twain's *Huckleberry Finn*, while written to cast a black adolescent in the role of a hero, perpetuates stereotypes humiliating to blacks. (See Reading 5.)

In 1967, The National Education Association called upon the publishing industry to "remove all distorted and inaccurate material about Negroes, American Indians, and other minorities from textbooks and other teaching material" and to "present an accurate and comprehensive portrayal of the cultural, economic, and scientific contributions—past and present—of all segments of American Society."[6]

## Churches

The more basic structures of the Protestant and Catholic church have inadvertently helped to create and establish the fixed racial attitudes that confront us today. It was written that the black skin was a punishment cast upon Cain and Ham and, consequently, on all their descendants. Symbolic reasoning through use of color helped to further separate honest reasoning from the religious approach. Religious paintings used the color yellow to signify cowardice and treason, and white and black to separate good and evil. An artistic expression of purity demanded the use of white: angels with white flowing robes and blond appearances, the white holy light of heaven, and the pure whiteness of the Holy Spirit.

Black, on the other hand, was the Christian's way of defining evil: the black pit of hell, the black soul of the devil, and the blackness of sin. It takes very little thought to connect this type of instruction with the structure of racism of today. Jesus, although a dark-skinned man with the dark hair of the Semite, was entirely reconstructed by the church. When he reemerged, he was a white, blue-eyed blond with all the "favorable" characteristics acceptable to the racist beliefs of the church. It was impossible to accept a dark Christ when dark signified evil. The same belief is expressed today. The remark, "his skin is black, but his soul is white," is sometimes heard. And since the church used yellow to designate cowardice and treason, have we not extended this concept to fit people of Oriental descent?

Many of the teachings of the Christian church also encourage anti-Semitism. Jews were blamed for the crucifixion of Jesus. The liturgy of the church cast the Jews in an inferior and despised position. During the Middle Ages, the Catholic Church discouraged association of Christians with Jews and the Crusades themselves became vehicles for the destruction of Jewish communities under the guise of seeking to rescue Jerusalem from the Moslem. Even Luther, who broke with the Catholic Church to launch the Protestant Reformation, became deeply anti-Semitic when he discovered that Jews would not accept Protestantism any more than they had previously accepted Catholicism. Today, in the spirit of ecumenism and under the leadership of Pope John XXIII many of the unjust references to the Jews in Catholic liturgy have been eliminated; but the damage remains. At various periods the church sent missionaries to impose Christianity on the pagan slave, the black man, and the Indian. In time, the church went through a reconstruction period, and the dark-skinned people were given the privilege of owning a soul, but by then the damage had been done, and the church had made a major contribution to racism. (See Reading 6.)

## Armed Forces

Racism is present in every branch of the American armed forces. Whenever a call to arms has sounded, thousands of black men have stepped forward and volunteered their services to protect a society that rejected them. Yet, in the armed forces, they have been relegated largely to service positions and, until recent years, were segregated into black units.

"Me? . . . I'm only on my way to save democracy in Vietnam!" (Yardley in The Baltimore Sun)

Demonstrators protesting the draft for service in Vietnam.
(Berne Greene)

Although today blacks have been integrated into all phases of the armed forces, they still feel the stigma of racism.

*The New York Times* (October 6, 1970) reported that racial outbursts, acts of sabotage—believed to be racially motivated—and cross burnings occurred among the 185,000 United States troops stationed in West Germany. As a result, the Pentagon sent a team to investigate the racial issue and to check into the newly formed black unity and defense groups, such as the Unsatisfied Black Soldiers, the Black United Soldiers, the Black Action Group. These and other groups formed to end discrimination within the military, believing that "no black is free until all blacks are free." Their beliefs and goals resemble in many ways the aims of black student groups in America. But here the parallel ends, for their members are soldiers, not students. As soldiers, it is their duty to kill or die for this country. One black sergeant said, "I've bled for my country way off in Nam. Now, if need be, I'll bleed for myself—for my people." A black officer commented, "You don't solve the racial problems of the American army in Europe by putting chitterlings and Afro-Sheen in the commissary. The problem will not end among our troops until it ends in America." And a white noncommissioned officer said, "Race is my problem, not the Russians, not Vietnam, Jordan, nor manuevers. I just worry about keeping my troops—black and white—from getting at one another. I just don't understand the race thing."

Superman of the "super" culture: reinforcement of the idea of white racial superiority.  (Joe Molnar)

*Mass Media*

The mass media have played a large part in the racial development of our thinking. Consider the magnitude of exposure that was and still is available to the film industry. For years the "good guys" wore white and the "bad guys" wore black. Whenever a band of Indians appeared, the captive audience always feared for the white settlers' safety.

Black men were depicted as shuffling, slow-thinking baboons who were inherently frightened of everything that moved. Movies usually portrayed the black in a menial and servile role—a porter, servant, or native in jungle countries. Those who watched films adopted to some degree the philosophy propounded on the screen; many went home believing that all blacks were slow-witted clowns. Today, in many movies, the black man emerges as a hero, but only in the context of white, middle-class values. (See Reading 7.)

Television commercials also perpetuate these values. We do see some blacks in television commercials only because they have fought, as consumers, for such representation. We rarely, if ever, see Spanish-speaking minority members in commercials. Discriminatory hiring practices, although gradually breaking down, continue to place the lion's share of media editing in the hands of white men. Today in the mass media there is a move toward eliminating racism. Such programs as "Sesame Street" portray children of all groups learning and playing together. In buses and on trains posters are prominently displayed depicting peoples of all races, colors, and creeds working in harmony.

THE CITY COMMISSION ON HUMAN RIGHTS JOHN V.

A New York City Commission on Human Rights poster displayed on buses. (Redmond, Marcus and Shure, Inc., for the City of New York Commission on Human Rights.)

White is beautiful.
Black is beautiful.
Yellow is beautiful.

# People is beautiful.

DSAY. MAYOR / SIMEON GOLAR. CHAIRMAN

## Industry

Labor and industry have done their share to perpetuate racial inequities by trapping minorities in
poverty. For years, only a minute percentage of
minorities was elevated above the blue-collar level.
As prosperity rose for whites, nonwhites made less
significant gains. Today, the large majority of menial,
low-income jobs are held by Puerto Ricans, blacks,
Mexicans, and Indians. Several studies commis-
sioned by the government found that discrimination,
not education or training, was the major reason
nonwhite income is lower than white income. "The
lower educational level of some minority groups is
a factor in their lower occupational status, but statis-
tical analyses using two different approaches show
that it accounts for only about one-third of the difference in occupational ranking between Negro men
and majority group men; the inevitable conclusion
is that the other two-thirds must be attributed to
discrimination, deliberate or inadvertent."[7] (See
Reading 8, Part A.) The Kerner Commission found
that unemployment and underemployment are the
most persistent and most serious grievances in minority areas. Blacks hold 63.5 percent of the menial
jobs, only 6 percent of professional or technical ones,
and 3 percent of business and sales jobs.

Other studies have shown that a white dropout
earns more than a nonwhite high school graduate.
"The median income for a Negro college graduate is
only $5,020; that is $110 less than the earnings of
white male high school dropouts. . . . A white high
school graduate may expect to earn $253,000 during
his lifetime, while a Negro with five or more years
of college may expect to earn only $246,000."[8]

What has happened to the spirit and dignity of

Ads for Spanish-speaking applicants. (Berne Greene)

Trapped in a menial job.    (Berne Greene)

those who are victims of economic racism? The poor white believes he can raise himself economically, but the nonwhite believes that American racism confines him to a low status, and that all channels of economic opportunity are blocked at every entrance. This feeling of conspiracy and rejection leads nonwhites first to humiliation, then apathy, and finally to the personal and social ills of narcotics addiction, crime, mental and physical illness, family breakdown, and suicide.

This overall picture of subhuman existence makes one think of a machine that mass produces defective gears which can never fit into the fine machinery of society. The longer we—as a nation and as individuals—are racially motivated, the longer American prosperity suffers. Faced with these dilemmas, can we ever become the "Great Society" without making a concerted effort to wipe out racism?

*Housing*

White racism by both individuals and the housing industry is the major reason for segregated housing. Many whites protest against racism, but they move out as soon as a nonwhite moves in next door. (See Reading 8, Part B.) The real estate industry argues that blacks and Puerto Ricans moving into a neighborhood will cause a decline in property values. Many zoning laws restrict the building of homes under a certain price level to ensure against minorities moving into the area, since the average income of minorities is substandard. In some deeds governing the sale and resale of a private home may be found clauses excluding people with "swarthy skins" which attempt in this way to retain the racial homogeneity of the community. While the grossest

practices of this kind are unlawful under federal
and state laws, deeply rooted traditions persist; even
today, blacks cannot select their homes or apartments as freely as whites, and Jews are still excluded
from some of the more prestigious communities in
the country.

The Jew, however, is a reasonably affluent minority, and is often able to penetrate this more affluent
environment. But if enough Jews move into the neighborhood, this may spur a migratory reaction among
the Gentiles. The neighborhood now becomes a
Jewish one, and the affluent black becomes the
threatening minority and the prime target of racism.

Financial institutions are well aware of the risk
of extending credit to minorities because of the depressing problems confronting these groups. The
near impossibility of finding economic security in
the social structure makes them prime risks. Thus,
for years banks refused or were extremely reluctant
to issue mortgages to blacks and other minorities.
However, some banks were willing to lend money
to minorities who wanted to purchase property in
traditional or transitional areas rather than in all-
white neighborhoods.

In recent years, civil rights organizations and the
federal government have tried several strategies to
combat racist practices in housing. One organization
—the Urban League—has dedicated itself to fair
housing, for it realizes that segregated housing means
segregated schools. And segregated schools ensure
that minorities will remain unprepared to enter the
mainstream of white America. Until segregation in
housing is obliterated, minorities will remain in
menial jobs, dependent on welfare programs, or un-
employed. Their family life will continue to be

Menial jobs lead to substandard housing.

An "old country" Jew walks in his urban ghetto. (Joe Molnar)

unstable and, as the population increases, more uneducated children will be raised.

One of the approaches of the Urban League is to send a white verifier to apply for a vacant apartment after a nonwhite applicant has been told that there are no apartments available. If the white verifier is rented or offered an apartment, he then becomes an irrefutable witness in a court action to prove that the nonwhite applicant was a victim of racism.

The government has issued an executive order prohibiting discrimination in federally owned housing and in new housing built with federal assistance. In the Civil Rights Act of 1964, another executive order permitted the government to cut off funds in any program where discrimination is found. In 1968, the government passed a law forbidding discrimination in the sale or rental of housing except for buildings with two to four units in which the owner makes his home. The law also forbids discrimination by banks and other lending institutions; discrimination in the conditions of sale, rental, or financing; discriminatory real estate services; and the use of threats or interference with a person exercising his rights under the law. Whether or not this law will be meaningful depends on how effectively it is enforced.

How Has Racism Affected Jews?

The infamy of anti-Semitism can be traced through many centuries to the present. Think of the Jew, and you think of the ghetto. Ghetto! The word itself conjures up dark and ugly shadows from the past. The ghetto was the place to which Jews were confined in the cities of medieval Europe. They lived out their lives in conditions not unlike those of today's slums, dressed often in distinctive garb, restricted in the ways in which they could make a living. With the French Revolution and the Enlightenment, most legal restrictions under which Jews lived were gradually lifted. The social stigma encouraged by racial bigotry remained.

Indeed, during the Hitler era, the most vicious crimes were once again committed against the Jews. Once again they were required to wear distinctive garb and display bright yellow badges to designate their shameful identity. Hitler's plan to wipe out the Jews is known as the crime of genocide—the killing of a people. Before he was defeated, Hitler had conquered much of central Europe, and genocide was practiced wherever his troops marched. By the time World War II ended, six million Jews had been slaughtered in the notorious gas chambers of Buchenwald, Auschwitz, Dachau, and other concentration camps. Even time cannot be the healing agent it usually is. Although the ugliness that was yesterday is put away in the dim recess of his memories, the Jew can never forget his long night of terror.

Today, Jews are part of the social structure of this country. Although they are not yet entirely accepted, they have reached a degree of greater affluence and less discomfort. An affluent Chicago woman reports: "I [am] a third-generation American. I am also Jewish, part of a 5000-year-old culture. My religion teaches me to love learning, to cherish family ties, to be my brother's keeper . . . [But] it has not been easy to be a Jew in this most free of all countries. In my high school there were social clubs no Jew was ever asked to join. I thought it would be different with me—my friends and I were so close—but it wasn't. It was difficult getting through the teen years—those hurts didn't help.

"Just a few years ago my husband and I came home to find 'Damn Jew' scrawled on our front door. Our sons have been called 'dirty Jew' in school. . . . I recognize there are still barriers. Jews cannot buy the home they want in some suburbs; whole companies still do not employ Jews no matter how qualified they are."[9]

Jews have been successful in business, in politics, and in the world of artistic and professional endeavor. Some have been extremely successful. Others are first beginning to feel a measure of security in the jobs they hold and in the niche in society they have but recently won for themselves. As blacks cry for "black power," and as they, too, press for their fair share of positions in business and in government, the ones who must make room for them are the most recent arrivals. These are usually the Jews and other immigrants who have just "made it."

## What Is Black Anti-Semitism?

As the cry for black power is heard, extreme anti-Jewish feelings are emerging among the black masses. Blacks resent exploitation by Jewish landlords and merchants which first created black resentment toward Jews. This attitude is considered by some black leaders not one of anti-Semitism but an expression of a new sense of identity among black Americans. Some Jewish leaders label this attitude "economic anti-Semitism."

Bayard Rustin neither apologizes nor tries to explain away black anti-Semitism. "It is here, it is dangerous, it must be rooted out. . . . What we can and had better do is to understand it if we are in fact to deal with it . . ."[10] Lucy S. Davidowicz, interpreting black-Jewish relations, says: "The poor

do pay more. . . . In Harlem Jewish grocers charge
more than in Forest Hills, so do Greek grocers and
Safeway markets. . . . Their expenses are higher . . . ;
risks are greater to property and even to life. . . .
Except that at the corner the grocer is accessible
and, if he is a Jew, vulnerable, the object of familiar
prejudices. Still, the Jewish grocer gives credit, while
A&P and Safeway do not."[11] Jews, who have had
a long history of oppression, resent black expressions of anti-Semitism, and many are withdrawing
their moral and financial support from the black
struggle.

Blacks and Jews have gone through an endless
time of suffering. Both have been subjected to degradation and humiliation from racists, and both have
witnessed the slaughter of their brothers. It is ironic
that the two groups most alienated, most discriminated against in modern times, find themselves
discriminating against each other. Perhaps they have
fallen into a cultural trap in their drive toward
recognition in this society. Bigotry is a well-rooted
part of American culture. By utilizing the same approach as that of their bigoted countrymen, some
may believe that they will thus be less conspicuous
and more acceptable. Bigotry may be said to resemble a ladder on which every group is given a
rung based on his ethnic background. The lower
rungs are reserved to those regarded as least socially
acceptable. What is to be gained if the blacks and
the Jews enter into conflict when the end result
will still find both groups at the foot of the ladder?

How Has Racism Affected the Hispanic Americans?

Recently, the Mexican-American, or Chicano, inspired by the sweeping black movement, has spoken out against lack of status, inequalities under the law, and discrimination. Some leaders, taking their cue from black power groups, are identifying themselves as the brown people. In the Chicano communities—barrios—the people are asking for a more active role in determining their future.

For years they have been aware that their community has been isolated from the mainstream of American life. As a result, the Chicanos have adopted self-protective measures (of speaking mostly in Spanish; noninvolvement in community affairs) to avoid feeling inadequate.

Chicanos helped to settle the West, build railroads, irrigation systems, and industry. Yet, where in our schools do we learn of their contributions to the development of our country?

Chicanos number about seven million. They live mainly in Arizona, California, Colorado, New Mexico, and Texas. The largest concentration of Mexican-Americans may be found in Los Angeles. Although a minority group, Chicanos have roots in America that go back long before the *Mayflower*. Since their origin is mainly Indian, they share with the American Indian the historical fact that they, more than others, were indeed the first Americans. It was the war with Mexico which ended in the defeat of that country in 1848 that marked Mexican-Americans as a defeated people. Their lands were taken from them and their labor was exploited. Though native to America, they speak Spanish as their first language and often find obstacles to success in

Chicanos working in the fields. (Wide World)

A group of poverty-stricken Chicano children. (Ed Lettau)

Mexican-American farm laborers, led by Cesar Chavez, picket a Safeway Supermarket in Seattle, Washington. (Wide World)

work and schooling doubly difficult because of the language barrier, and related socioeconomic factors.

Tiring of poverty, segregation, and rejection of their language by the dominant society, Chicano farm laborers are becoming more militant and have organized strikes to bring publicity to their plight. In Los Angeles, there is a very militant group called the Brown Berets. Their brown berets symbolize brown power ideals, just as the militant black power groups raise their left hand in a clenched fist as a symbol of their ideals as they cry "Power to the People." Are these emphases on colors rather than on cultures another form of racism? (See Reading 9.)

As the Chicanos constitute a Spanish-speaking native minority in the American Southwest, the Puerto Ricans and Cubans constitute a Spanish-speaking migrant minority mainly in the American Northeast. When in 1898 America won the war against Spain, Puerto Rico became a possession of the United States. Through subsequent legislation passed by Congress in 1917, the inhabitants of Puerto Rico were made citizens of the United States. It is as citizens that they can continue to go back and

A group of Puerto Ricans playing their native music.    (Joe Molnar)

forth between the mainland and the island as they
wish. As immigration from Western Europe was
cut off, Puerto Rican migration began to grow in
the 1920s and such migration from the island has
been a major source of newcomers to America ever
since. Although New York has the largest concentration of Puerto Ricans, large numbers are also
found in Philadelphia, Chicago, Pittsburgh, San Francisco, and Los Angeles. Cubans fleeing the dictatorial regime in their country have migrated to
Florida and to the New York area as well. The
Hispanic Americans, especially Puerto Ricans, are a
very mixed people because of intermarriage between
Caucasians and Negroes. These people are a good
example of why it is difficult to classify mankind
into races. The Puerto Ricans and Cubans, upon ar-
rival in the United States, have suddenly had to face a
form of prejudice unknown in their islands. Although
they had problems in their native environments and
are at least making a living here, their labor is tre-
mendously exploited and their dignity destroyed. (See
Reading 8.)

How Has Racism Affected the Indians?

Another group that has been the object of great
discrimination is the American Indians. Beginning
with mass murders and the seizure of their lands, as
was mentioned earlier, these people have endured
over three centuries of oppression. The small number who have survived have been forced onto gov-
ernment-controlled reservations and subjugated to
the culture of the invaders. The Indians—the original
Americans—have had United States education and
culture thrust upon them and yet have not had suffi-
cient opportunity to get decent employment. Many

A tepee representing Indian occupation of Alcatraz in November, 1969. An old treaty gave Indians rights to unused Federal property. (Alan Copeland in The New York Times)

of these people are living at a bare subsistence level, suspended between two worlds—uprooted from their agricultural and pastoral ways of life and unable to succeed in modern American society. In a land espousing freedom of religion Indians have even been arrested for practicing their ancient cults simply because their ceremonies involve taking medicinal drugs.

Recently Indians have been rebelling and there have been demonstrations and militant activities in many states aimed at the preservation of tradition

Teen-age demonstrators inspecting prison galleries on Alcatraz in February, 1970. They were attempting to secure the right to build an Indian education and cultural center there. (UPI)

and the restoration of ancestral lands. On the east coast one Indian group has formed an organization called Defenders of the American Indians, which is trying to get the government to let them redevelop their reservation properties and use these for building private business establishments. (See Reading 10.)

A Menominee Indian stands with shotgun ready at the gate of an abandoned Nike missile site on Chicago's lakefront, in July, 1971. Chicago police later stormed the base amid rocks and fire bombs to recapture it. (UPI)

Black power symbolized militantly at a Black Panther rally
and . . .                                          (Berne Greene)

## What Are the Damaging Results of Racism?

One obvious result of racism is the smoldering hatred that many nonwhites have for whites. After generations of abuse, the hatred of one generation was compounded by the hatred of the next and so on. The end result is what we see today. Riots and looting by blacks have cost this country millions of dollars and have further divided us into opposing camps. Other minority groups are joining in the crusade for equal rights. An increasing number of nonwhite middle-class citizens are becoming more militant.

artistically by young blacks on a neighborhood wall.   (Joe Molnar)

Minority groups are making more and more demands for separate control of their schools and communities. The cry for "black power," "Indian power," "Chicano power," "Puerto Rican power" is being heard more and more across the nation. Is this not racism in reverse? What are the social and personal consequences of such beliefs?

Another result of racism is that whites are becoming more fearful of mass demonstrations, even those that are held within the framework of the law. Many whites admit to feeling uneasy on the street, and whites and nonwhites alike are arming their homes as if for warfare.

After 1965, when the blacks began to cry for black power, public support for civil rights waned and an increase in white backlash was felt across the country. Whites, particularly the poorer ones, felt that the blacks were impatient and exerting too much pressure to get too much too soon.

Blacks, well aware of an increase in resistance, became more determined to overcome all obstacles that prevent them from having decent homes, schools, and jobs.

The majority of both sides is keenly aware that America is in a crisis, and they are committed to a nonviolent solution. There is, however, a powerful minority—white and black—who believes that a violent racial explosion is the solution.

Whites may wish that the black revolt will wane and die, but blacks are committed to finding equality under the law. Today the moderate black leaders are faced with a dilemma: (1) how to regain lost white support because their problems cannot be solved without it, and (2) how to prevent the militant leaders from gaining more support.

A martyred hero in the battle against racism: Martin Luther
King (1929–1968).   (Wide World)

What Is Being Done About Racism?

Today there is a move toward eliminating racism from our society. In dramatic efforts to bring about its demise, the government, private groups, and individuals have launched an attack in almost every area where racism abounds. Mythical fears and old wives' tales handed down for generations are being exploded. Young and old are being reeducated to make an honest appraisal of the shortcomings of rejection and unfounded bias against any ethnic group.

First, we have been willing to admit to ourselves and others that America is a racist society. Senator Abraham A. Ribicoff said: "The plain fact is that racism is rampant throughout the country. . . . The institutional roots of racism—which depersonalize our prejudices and make it easier for us to defend them—are as deeply embedded in the large metropolitan communities of the North as they are in the small rural communities of the South. . . . Massive school segregation does not exist because we have segregated our schools but because we have segregated our society and our neighborhoods. That is the source of the inequality, the tension and the hatred that disfigure our nation. . . ."[12]

Secondly, new organizations across the nation have formed to develop educational and direct-action programs to combat racism. One is a nonprofit group funded by church and foundation groups—the Committee for One Society (COS). Located in Chicago, COS provides consulting services to companies and institutions on methods to eliminate policies directed against minority groups. In California, a coalition of the Valley Interfaith Commission, the San Fernando

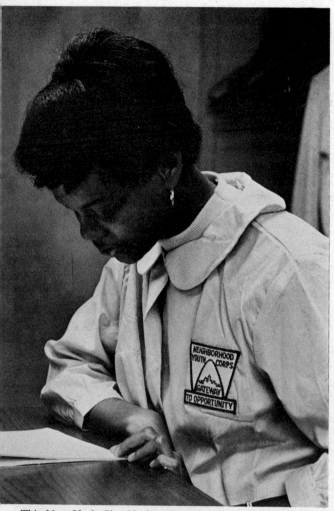

This New York City black girl was one of a group placed in jobs by the St. Louis Youth Corps. She proofreads an employee manual at a Jewish Center, improving her reading skill while doing secretarial work. (Black Star)

Valley Fair Housing Council, the Neighborhood Action Corporation, and Join Hands works together to support demands for change by the black and brown communities.

Join Hands, which began after Dr. Martin Luther King's assassination, stresses individual action. Members urge homeowners who want to sell to consider selling to minority families, talk to store managers about hiring minority employees, and speak to bank managers about lending money to minority businesses. Some members involve themselves in encounter groups which discuss racial attitudes and values.

In Washington, D.C., Protestant, Roman Catholic, and Jewish agencies are supporting the Metropoli-

Through private and government funds, minority group youth are finally gaining access to college educations. (Shelly Rusten)

tan Ecumenical Training Center (METC) which is attempting to provide leadership training and skills needed to combat institutional racism from within and without.

Other recently formed antiracist organizations are Fellowship of Racial and Economic Equality (FREE), Lynchburg, Virginia; National People Against Racism (PAR), Detroit, Michigan; Action Training Coalition (ATC), New York, New York; Suburban Action Center, Jenkintown, Pennsylvania.

Long-established organizations such as the Ford Foundation are giving financial aid to minority groups: grants of $2.7 million have been awarded to 48 colleges and universities across the country which have made efforts to encourage blacks, Puerto Ricans, and Mexicans to enroll. This money will be used to provide counseling services and to strengthen curricula for minority students. For example, in San Francisco, Chicano college students will be given instructions in English, and in Mississippi the funds will be used to recruit high school seniors for college.

The youth of today, acutely aware that America has not put into practice the ideals of humanity and justice for all, are so disillusioned that they feel morally justified in using whatever approach they may feel is necessary to call to their predecessors' attention the crying need for change. Some approaches are destructive—rioting, burning of property, inflammatory speeches—but the larger majority approach the problem with realistic constructiveness. They are not afraid to question the credibility of white middle-class values; they are not afraid to intermarry; they question the church's stand on racism and the validity of our educational institutions. They are willing to confront the government for its malfeasance even in the face of imprisonment.

Demonstrators voice disapproval of the trial of thirteen Black Panthers charged with conspiracy to bomb public places in New York and with attempted murder and arson. (UPI)

Many white young adult couples who fought prejudice at home are making a determined effort to break the cycle of the sins of the fathers being visited upon the sons. They, as parents, take every opportunity to instill in the minds of their children a compassionate desire to create a society that will not support racism in any form.

As white America offers her hand on equal terms, nonwhites must set aside their mistrust and hatred of the whites and offer their hands in return. To live together in harmony, both groups must accept differences in color, religion, cultures, and heritages.

Whites and blacks work together to solve community problems. (Ed Lettau)

# Part Two

# Selected Readings

Many people believe that a person's physical, moral, mental, and emotional traits are determined by his race, and that some races are superior to others. Thus these racists argue that intermarriage or race mixture will introduce inferior qualities into the bloodstream of the superior race, thereby reducing them to a lower level of humanity. The author of this selection, a noted anthropologist, discusses the relationship between race, intelligence, and culture.

# 1

## "Race," Intelligence and Culture

by ASHLEY MONTAGU

THE POPULAR VIEW of "race" has it that "race" and intelligence are linked, that certain types of bodies go with certain types of minds. Is this so? The answer is that in spite of numerous studies and investigations specifically designed to discover whether

From "Race, Intelligence and Culture," in *What We Know about Race*, by Ashley Montagu (New York: The One Nation Library, the Anti-Defamation League of B'nai B'rith, 1968), pp. 14–17. Copyright © 1968 by B'nai B'rith. Reprinted by permission.

any such linkage exists, no one has ever been able to demonstrate that they do. It is to be feared, in fact, that many investigators have set out with the firm intention of discovering such linkages. This is, of course, not the scientific way of doing things. A genuine scientist is not interested in setting out to find anything to be either one way or the other. He isn't interested in proving this or that theory. What he is concerned with is in discovering what *is,* in discovering how things actually are, and then stating them, no matter where the chips may fall. . . .

But no one has ever denied that differences exist between the ethnic groups of mankind. There are scores of such differences. The real point, however, is whether those differences are "racial" or not. And if not, to what then are such differences due?

Before we go a step further it is necessary to say that no one claims that some differences in intelligence may not exist between different ethnic groups. Such differences may very well exist. It is probable that they do. For no two groups when compared with one another are ever exactly alike in any of the respects in which they are compared, just as no two individuals are ever exactly alike. But this is a very different thing from saying that ethnic groups differ considerably from one another with respect to intelligence. There is no evidence whatever for such a statement, in spite of many attempts to find that evidence. On the contrary, the evidence that most scientists agree upon indicates that between one ethnic group and another the biological endowment for intelligence is much the same. And by intelligence is meant *the ability to make a successful response to a situation.*

When you compare the intelligence of two people remember that what you are doing is not comparing

These South American village children might have a high
capacity for learning, but would our present tests measure
their true potential intelligence?   (Ed Lettau)

the native intelligence, the biological endowment for intelligence. Rather, you are comparing the opportunities for the development of that biological endowment as expressed in the intelligence of the two individuals.

Intelligence just doesn't grow of itself. It has to be stimulated, and it is generally stimulated in a particular environment by particular people. Suppose you were born in a small village in a land in which there is great poverty and where the illiteracy rate is high. At your present age you wouldn't be able to read or write. You would probably believe in all sorts of fantastic things, such as that diseases are sent by demons and can be brought on by the evil eye, that flies are created by decaying rubbish, and that the sun travels around the earth. Compared to yourself as you are at the present time, with all the advantages of having been born and brought up and gone to school in the United States, your "village" self would be very stupid, indeed. And yet, the two of you would be one and the same person. Why, then, is your "village" self stupid and your American self intelligent?

The answer is that your "village" self was brought up in one way of life, while your American self was brought up in another, with all the advantages of a high standard of living and the benefits of a highly developed educational system. In short, the *opportunities* for the development of your intelligence would be more favorable in America than they would be in the village, and that is the only reason why your American self would be superior in intelligence to your "village" self. Your biological endowment for intelligence would have been the same, but your social opportunities for the development of that intelligence would have been different; hence your intelligence would have expressed itself differently.

Suppose you were living in America a hundred years ago on a farmstead, and when you were little you were captured by the Indians, and lived with them for the rest of your life. Do you think you would have grown up as a white or as an Indian? I can tell you because we know the answer with complete certainty: You would have grown up as an Indian. For this experience actually befell many white children, some of whom were later discovered as adolescents or adults. . . .

The interesting thing about these white Indians is that after living for years with Indian tribes they were unwilling to return to the white way of life. And, not only did they act like Indians, but it was consistently remarked that they even looked like Indians. This is quite understandable because the face, to a large extent, is an index of the mind, and the thoughts and feelings one habitually indulges in leave a permanent record in the expressions of the face.

The opportunities afforded these white children were to become Indians, and Indians they became. The same would have happened to you or me under similar circumstances. . . .

There are many ways of life that are different from ours.

Most people in the world sleep on the ground. Hundreds of millions use a piece of wood for a pillow. Millions of others consider milk a disgusting liquid. Millions are unable to read or add. Some groups make clicks when they speak, others whistle, some never wear any clothes, others conceal virtually every conceivable part of the body, and so on. Are these traits "racial" or are they due to the ways of life of these peoples? Some have claimed that such traits are racial. It is, in fact, not difficult to show that they are not "racial" at all, but due to the way of life in which each of these peoples have been brought up—as in the case of the white Indians. . . . The way of life is what the anthropologist—the student of man—calls *culture*. The question is: What is the most important thing in influencing the development of intelligence, "race" or culture?

By applying the test of *opportunity* whenever the matter of the comparative intelligence of persons or of people arises you will find that you have in your power a fine instrument for screening out the factors that are probably responsible for the difference in the intelligence as you observe it. . . .

The thing to understand is that there is no intelligence without the stimulation of the environment. Therefore, intelligence is the expression of the interaction between biological endowment and the opportunities afforded by the stimulus of the environment. What people know and do, assuming the general similarity of the biological endowment for intelligence, will largely depend upon the opportunities afforded them by their environment. One has to learn to learn, and one has to learn to be intelligent. . . .

In this selection Gertrude Bonnin, a
Dakota Sioux Indian, brings out dramat-
ically the pathos of the American Indian's plight. Although Indians today
are making some progress toward
restoration of their lost culture, how can
any social action erase the hatred
generated by memories such as these?

# 2

# Impressions of an Indian Childhood

by GERTRUDE BONNIN (ZITKALA-SA)

A WIGWAM of weather-stained canvas stood at the
base of some irregularly ascending hills. A footpath
wound its way gently down the sloping land till it
reached the broad river bottom; creeping through
the long swamp grasses that bent over it on either
side, it came out on the edge of the Missouri.

From *A Nation of Nations, Ethnic Literature in America*,
edited by Theodore L. Gross (New York: The Free Press),
pp. 160–62. Copyright © 1971 by The Free Press.

Here, morning, noon, and evening, my mother came to draw water from the muddy stream for our household use. Always, when my mother started for the river, I stopped my play to run along with her. She was only of medium height. Often she was sad and silent, at which times her full arched lips were compressed into hard and bitter lines, and shadows fell under her black eyes. Then I clung to her hand and begged to know what made the tears fall.

"Hush; my little daughter must never talk about my tears"; and smiling through them, she patted my head and said, "Now let me see how fast you can run today." Whereupon I tore away at my highest possible speed, with my long black hair blowing in the breeze.

I was a wild little girl of seven. Loosely clad in a slip of brown buckskin, and lightfooted with a pair of soft moccasins on my feet, I was as free as the wind that blew my hair, and no less spirited than a bounding deer. These were my mother's pride—my wild freedom and overflowing spirits. She taught me no fear save that of intruding myself upon others.

Having gone many paces ahead I stopped, panting for breath, and laughing with glee as my mother watched my every movement. I was not wholly conscious of myself, but was more keenly alive to the fire within. It was as if I were the activity, and my hands and feet were only experiments for my spirit to work upon.

Returning from the river, I tugged beside my mother, with my hand upon the bucket I believed I was carrying. One time, on such a return, I remember a bit of conversation we had. My grown-up cousin, Warca-Ziwin (Sunflower), who was then seventeen, always went to the river alone for water for her mother. Their wigwam was not far from ours;

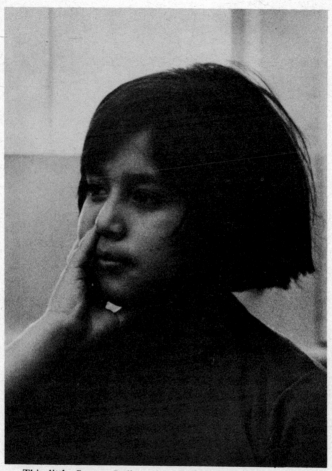

This little Seneca Indian girl of New York State today is still facing the problems of white domination. (Burt Shavitz)

and I saw her daily going to and from the river. I admired my cousin greatly. So I said: "Mother, when I am tall as my cousin Warca-Ziwin, you shall not have to come for water. I will do it for you."

With a strange tremor in her voice which I could not understand, she answered, "If the paleface does not take away from us the river we drink."

"Mother, who is this bad paleface?" I asked.

"My little daughter, he is a sham,—a sickly sham! The bronzed Dakota is the only real man."

I looked up into my mother's face while she spoke; and seeing her bite her lips, I knew she was unhappy. This aroused revenge in my small soul. Stamping my foot on the earth, I cried aloud, "I hate the paleface that makes my mother cry!"

Setting the pail of water on the ground, my mother stooped, and stretching her left hand out on the level with my eyes, she placed her other arm about me; she pointed to the hill where my uncle and my only sister lay buried.

"There is what the paleface has done! Since then your father too has been buried in a hill nearer the rising sun. We were once very happy. But the paleface has stolen our lands and driven us hither. Having defrauded us of our land, the paleface forced us away.

"Well, it happened on the day we moved camp that your sister and uncle were both very sick. Many others were ailing, but there seemed to be no help. We traveled many days and nights; not in the grand, happy way that we moved camp when I was a little girl, but we were driven, my child, driven like a herd of buffalo. With every step, your sister, who was not as large as you are now, shrieked with the painful jar until she was hoarse with crying. She grew more and more feverish. Her little hands and

Uprooted from their peaceful and natural dwellings . . .
(Burt Shavitz)

these New York Seneca Indians were forced to sell their
land for the building of a dam and move into project
houses which they dislike. (Burt Shavitz)

cheeks were burning hot. Her little lips were parched
and dry, but she would not drink the water I gave
her. Then I discovered that her throat was swollen
and red. My poor child, how I cried with her because the Great Spirit had forgotten us!

"At last, when we reached this western country,
on the first weary night your sister died. And soon
your uncle died also, leaving a widow and an orphan
daughter, your cousin Warca-Ziwin. Both your sister
and uncle might have been happy with us today, had
it not been for the heartless paleface."

My mother was silent the rest of the way to our
wigwam. Though I saw no tears in her eyes, I knew
that was because I was with her. She seldom wept
before me.

In the 1920s our immigration policy changed from unlimited to limited immigration—the quota system. Long before our concern about European immigration, Congress prohibited Chinese immigration. In 1882 Congress passed a Chinese Exclusion Act which decreed no more Chinese could immigrate to this country and that people born in China could not be naturalized.

In a speech delivered in Congress on February 28, 1882, Senator Miller expressed the feelings of many of his contemporaries who were against Chinese immigration. The excerpt below is an example of the sentiment of many of the nation's lawmakers of that time.

**3**

# "But Why This Discrimination Against the Chinese?"

by SENATOR JOHN FRANKLIN MILLER

. . . If we continue to permit the introduction of this strange people, with their peculiar civilization, until they form a considerable part of our popula-

From an Address by Senator John Franklin Miller (California, 1881–87), February 28, 1882. *Congressional Record* (Washington, D.C.: Government Printing Office).

Many immigrants do not find equal opportunities for fair
housing and decent jobs.  (Joe Molnar)

tion, what is to be the effect upon the American people and Anglo Saxon civilization? Can the two civilizations endure side by side as two distinct and hostile forces? . . . Can they meet half way, and so merge in a mongrel race, half Chinese and half Caucasian, as to produce a civilization half pagan, half Christian, semi-oriental, altogether mixed and very bad? . . . The presence of the Chinese has produced a labor system which is unique; at least different from that of any other part of the United States. This is seen in the wandering, unsettled habits of white farm laborers, who, forced into competition with the Chinese, have been compelled to adopt their nomadic habit. . . .

The new element in American society called the "hoodlum" is the result of Chinese competition in the manufacturing districts in California, by which young people of both sexes are driven to idleness in the streets. Strange and incurable maladies, loathsome and infectious diseases have been introduced which no medical skill can circumscribe or extirpate, and the stupefying, destructive opium habit is steadily increasing among our people.

. . . During the late depression in business affairs which existed for three or four years in California, while thousands of white men and women were walking the streets, begging and pleading for an opportunity to give their honest labor for any wages, the great steamers . . . discharged at the wharves of San Francisco their accustomed cargoes of Chinese. . . .

. . . they [the Chinese] never change or abandon their habits or methods no matter what their surroundings may be. They herd together like beasts in places where white men could not live; they clothe themselves in the cheapest raiment as they have done in China, and subsist on cheap food imported for their use and the refuse of our markets.

. . . But why this discrimination against the Chinese? It was because they are unfit for the responsibilities, duties, and privileges of American citizenship. . . . If they should be admitted to citizenship, then there would be a new element introduced into the governing power of this nation, which would be the most venal, irresponsible, ignorant, and vicious of all the bad elements which have been infused into the body-politic—an element disloyal to American institutions, inimical to republican liberty, scornful of American civilization, not fit for self-government and unfit to participate in the government of others—a people destitute of conscience or the moral sense. . . . They would esteem the suffrage only for the money they could make out of it.

Eldridge Cleaver, Black Panther Party Minister of Information and a former candidate for the Presidency of the United States on the Peace and Freedom Party ticket, wrote this selection while he was in California's Folsom State Prison. Here he examines the conflicting forces within America. He believes that "in the world revolution now under way, the initiative rests with people of color."

# 4

# The White Race and Its Heroes

by ELDRIDGE CLEAVER

FROM THE BEGINNING, America has been a schizo-phrenic nation. Its two conflicting images of itself were never reconciled, because never before has the survival of its most cherished myths made a recon-ciliation mandatory. Once before, during the bitter struggle between North and South climaxed by the

From *Soul on Ice*, by Eldridge Cleaver. Copyright © 1968 by Eldridge Cleaver. Reprinted by permission of McGraw-Hill Book Company, New York, and Jonathan Cape Ltd., London.

Eldridge Cleaver holding a news conference in Los Angeles after the University of California approved one lecture by him at the Berkeley campus in 1968. (Wide World)

Civil War, the two images of America came into conflict, although whites North and South scarcely understood it. The image of America held by its most alienated citizens was advanced neither by the North nor by the South; it was perhaps best expressed by Frederick Douglass, who was born into slavery in 1817, escaped to the North, and became the greatest leader-spokesman for the blacks of his era. In words that can still, years later, arouse an audience of black Americans, Frederick Douglass delivered, in 1852, a scorching indictment in his Fourth of July oration in Rochester:

What to the American slave is your Fourth of July? I answer: a day that reveals to him, more than all other days in the year, the gross injustice and cruelty to which he is the constant victim. To him your celebration is a sham; your boasted liberty, an unholy licence; your national greatness, swelling vanity; your sounds of rejoicing are empty and heartless; your denunciation of tyrants, brass-fronted impudence; your shouts of liberty and equality, hollow mockery; your prayers and hymns, your sermons and thanksgivings, with all your religious parade and solemnity, are, to him, more bombast, fraud, deception, impiety and hypocrisy—a thin veil to cover up crimes which would disgrace a nation of savages. . . .

You boast of your love of liberty, your superior civilization, and your pure Christianity, while the whole political power of the nation (as embodied in the two great political parties) is solemnly pledged to support and perpetuate the enslavement of three millions of your countrymen. You hurl your anathemas at the crown-headed tyrants of Russia and Austria and pride yourselves on your democratic institutions, while you yourselves consent to be the mere *tools* and *bodyguards* of the tyrants of Virginia and Carolina.

You invite to your shores fugitives of oppression from abroad, honor them with banquets, greet them with ovations, cheer them, toast them, salute them, protect them, and pour out your money to them like water; but the fugitive from your own land you advertise, hunt, arrest, shoot, and kill. You glory in your refinement and your universal education; yet you maintain a system as barbarous and dreadful as ever stained the character of a nation—a system begun in avarice, supported in pride, and perpetuated in cruelty.

You shed tears over fallen Hungary, and make the sad story of her wrongs the theme of your poets, statesmen and orators, till your gallant sons are ready to fly to arms to vindicate her cause against the oppressor; but, in regard to the ten thousand wrongs of the American slave, you would enforce the strictest silence, and would hail him as an enemy of the nation who dares to make these wrongs the subject of public discourse!

This most alienated view of America was preached by the Abolitionists, and by Harriet Beecher Stowe in her *Uncle Tom's Cabin*. But such a view of America was too distasteful to receive wide attention, and serious debate about America's image and her reality was engaged in only on the fringes of society. Even when confronted with overwhelming evidence to the contrary, most white Americans have found it possible, after steadying their rattled nerves, to settle comfortably back into their vaunted belief that America is dedicated to the proposition that all men are created equal and endowed by their Creator with certain inalienable rights—life, liberty and the pursuit of happiness. With the Constitution for a rudder and the Declaration of Independence as its guiding star, the ship of state is sailing always toward a brighter vision of freedom and justice for all.

Because there is no common ground between these two contradictory images of America, they had to be kept apart. But the moment the blacks were let into the white world—let out of the voiceless and faceless cages of their ghettos, singing, walking, talking, dancing, writing, and orating *their* image of America and of Americans—the white world was suddenly challenged to match its practice to its preachments. And this is why those whites who abandon the *white* image of America and adopt the *black* are greeted with such unmitigated hostility by their elders.

For all these years whites have been taught to believe in the myth they preached, while Negroes have had to face the bitter reality of what America practiced. But without the lies and distortions, white Americans would not have been able to do the things they have done. When whites are forced to look honestly upon the objective proof of their deeds, the cement of mendacity holding white society together swiftly disintegrates. On the other hand, the core of the black world's vision remains intact, and in fact begins to expand and spread into the psychological territory vacated by the non-viable white lies, i.e., into the minds of young whites. It is remarkable how the system worked for so many years, how the majority of whites remained effectively unaware of any contradiction between their view of the world and that world itself. The mechanism by which this was rendered possible requires examination at this point.

Let us recall that the white man, in order to justify slavery and, later on, to justify segregation, elaborated a complex, all-pervasive myth which at one time classified the black man as a subhuman beast of burden. The myth was progressively modified, gradually elevating the blacks on the scale of evolution, following their slowly changing status, until the plateau of separate-but-equal was reached at the close of the nineteenth century. During slavery, the black was seen as a mindless Supermasculine Menial. Forced to do the backbreaking work, he was conceived in terms of his ability to do such work—"field niggers," etc. The white man administered the plantation, doing all the thinking, exercising omnipotent power over the slaves. He had little difficulty dissociating himself from the black slaves, and he could not conceive of their positions being reversed or even reversible.

Blacks and whites being conceived as mutually exclusive types, those attributes imputed to the blacks could not also be imputed to the whites—at least not in equal degree—without blurring the line separating the races. These images were based upon the social function of the two races, the work they performed. The ideal white man was one who knew how to use his head, who knew how to manage and control things and get things done. Those whites who were not in a position to perform these functions nevertheless aspired to them. The ideal black man was one who did exactly as he was told, and did it efficiently and cheerfully. "Slaves," said Frederick Douglass, "are generally expected to sing as well as to work." As the black man's position and function became more varied, the images of white and black, having become stereotypes, lagged behind.

The separate-but-equal doctrine was promulgated

by the Supreme Court in 1896. It had the same purpose domestically as the Open Door Policy toward
China in the international arena: to stabilize a situation and subordinate a non-white population so that
racist exploiters could manipulate those people according to their own selfish interests. These doc-
trines were foisted off as *the epitome of enlightened
justice, the highest expression of morality.* Sanctified
by religion, justified by philosophy and legalized by
the Supreme Court, separate-but-equal was enforced
by day by agencies of the law, and by the KKK &
Co. under cover of night. Booker T. Washington, the
Martin Luther King of his day, accepted separate-
but-equal in the name of all Negroes. W. E. B.
DuBois denounced it.

Separate-but-equal marked the last stage of the
white man's flight into cultural neurosis, and the
beginning of the black man's frantic striving to
assert his humanity and equalize his position with
the white. Blacks ventured into all fields of endeavor to which they could gain entrance. Their goal
was to present in all fields a performance that would
equal or surpass that of the whites. It was long
axiomatic among blacks that a black had to be
twice as competent as a white in any field in order
to win grudging recognition from the whites. This
produced a pathological motivation in the blacks to
equal or surpass the whites, and a pathological motivation in the whites to maintain a distance from
the blacks. This is the rack on which black and white
Americans receive their delicious torture! At first
there was the color bar, flatly denying the blacks
entrance to certain spheres of activity. When this no
longer worked, and blacks invaded sector after sector
of American life and economy, the whites evolved
other methods of keeping their distance. The il-

lusion of the Negro's inferior nature had to be maintained.

One device evolved by the whites was to tab whatever the blacks did with the prefix "Negro." We had *Negro* literature, *Negro* athletes, *Negro* music, *Negro* doctors, *Negro* politicians, *Negro* workers. The malignant ingeniousness of this device is that although it accurately describes an objective biological fact—or, at least, a sociological fact in America—it concealed the paramount psychological fact: that to the white mind, prefixing anything with "Negro" automatically consigned it to an inferior category. A well-known example of the white necessity to deny due credit to blacks is in the realm of music. White musicians were famous for going to Harlem and other Negro cultural centers literally to steal the black man's music, carrying it back across the color line into the Great White World and passing off the watered-down loot as their own original creations. Blacks, meanwhile, were ridiculed as *Negro* musicians playing inferior coon music.

The Negro revolution at home and national liberation movements abroad have unceremoniously shattered the world of fantasy in which the whites have been living. It is painful that many do not yet see that their fantasy world has been rendered uninhabitable in the last half of the twentieth century. But it is away from this world that the white youth of today are turning. The "paper tiger" hero, James Bond, offering the whites a triumphant image of themselves, is saying what many whites want desperately to hear reaffirmed: *I am still the White Man, lord of the land, licensed to kill, and the world is still an empire at my feet.* James Bond feeds on that secret little anxiety, the psychological white backlash, felt in some degree by most whites alive.

It is exasperating to see little brown men and little yellow men from the mysterious Orient, and the opaque black men of Africa (to say nothing of these impudent American Negroes!) who come to the UN and talk smart to us, who are scurrying all over *our* globe in their strange modes of dress—much as if they were new, unpleasant arrivals from another planet. Many whites believe in their ulcers that it is only a matter of time before the Marines get the signal to round up these truants and put them back securely in their cages. But it is away from this fantasy world that the white youth of today are turning.

In the world revolution now under way, the initiative rests with people of color. That growing numbers of white youth are repudiating their heritage of blood and taking people of color as their heroes and models is a tribute not only to their insight but to the resilience of the human spirit.

Huck Finn with Jim.

This selection is from one of the great classics of American folk literature. It was long a favorite of teachers and students alike. Yet lately, in an era more sensitive to racial slights, the book has gradually fallen into disfavor and was removed from many reading lists and school library shelves. The question is whether a selection such as the one below can be read in the light of contemporary developments without compromising the views of the black minority and be used to further racial understanding for all men.

# 5

## The Adventures of Huckleberry Finn

by MARK TWAIN

WE WENT tiptoeing along a path amongst the trees back toward the end of the widow's garden, stooping down so as the branches wouldn't scrape our heads. When we was passing by the kitchen I fell over a root and made a noise. We scrouched down and laid still. Miss Watson's big nigger, named Jim, was set-

From "Our Gang's Dark Oath," Chapter II, *The Adventures of Huckleberry Finn,* by Mark Twain. Reprinted by permission of Harper & Row, Publishers, Inc.

ting in the kitchen door; we could see him pretty clear, because there was a light behind him. He got up and stretched his neck out about a minute, listening. Then he says:

"Who dah?"

He listened some more; then he came tiptoeing down and stood right between us; we could 'a' touched him, nearly. Well, likely it was minutes and minutes that there warn't a sound, and we all there so close together. There was a place on my ankle that got to itching, but I dasn't scratch it; and then my ear begun to itch; and next my back, right between my shoulders. Seemed like I'd die if I couldn't scratch. Well, I've noticed that thing plenty of times since. If you are with the quality, or at a funeral, or trying to go to sleep when you ain't sleepy—if you are anywheres where it won't do for you to scratch, why, you will itch all over in upward of a thousand places. Pretty soon Jim says:

"Say, who is you? Whar is you? Dog my cats ef I didn' hear sumf'n. Well, I know what I's gwyne to do: I's gwyne to set down here and listen tell I hears it ag'in."

So he set down on the ground betwixt me and Tom. He leaned his back up against a tree, and stretched his legs out till one of them most touched one of mine. My nose begun to itch. It itched till the tears come into my eyes. But I dasn't scratch. Then it begun to itch on the inside. Next I got to itching underneath. I didn't know how I was going to set still. This miserableness went on as much as six or seven minutes; but it seemed a sight longer than that. I was itching in eleven different places now. I reckoned I couldn't stand it more'n a minute longer, but I set my teeth hard and got ready to try. Just then Jim begun to breathe heavy; next he begun to snore—and then I was pretty soon comfortable again.

Tom he made a sign to me—kind of a little noise with his mouth—and we went creeping away on our hands and knees. When we was ten foot off Tom whispered to me, and wanted to tie Jim to the tree for fun. But I said no; he might wake and make a disturbance, and then they'd find out I warn't in. Then Tom said he hadn't got candles enough, and he would slip in the kitchen and get some more. I didn't want him to try. I said Jim might wake up and come. But Tom wanted to resk it; so we slid in there and got three candles, and Tom laid five cents on the table for pay. Then we got out, and I was in a sweat to get away; but nothing would do Tom but he must crawl to where Jim was, on his hands and knees, and play something on him. I waited, and it seemed a good while, everything was so still and lonesome.

As soon as Tom was back we cut along the path, around the garden fence, and by and by fetched up on the steep top of the hill the other side of the house. Tom said he slipped Jim's hat off of his head and hung it on a limb right over him, and Jim stirred a little, but he didn't wake. Afterward Jim said the witches bewitched him and put him in a trance, and rode him all over the state, and then set him under the trees again, and hung his hat on a limb to show who done it. And next time Jim told it he said they rode him down to New Orleans; and, after that, every time he told it he spread it more and more, till by and by he said they rode him all over the world, and tired him most to death, and his back was all over saddle boils. Jim was monstrous proud about it, and he got so he wouldn't hardly notice the other niggers. Niggers would come miles to hear Jim tell about it, and he was more looked up to than any nigger in that country. Strange niggers would stand with their mouths open and look him all over, same as if he was a wonder. Niggers is always talking about witches in the dark by the kitchen fire; but whenever one was talking and letting on to know all about such things, Jim would happen in and say, "Hm! What you know 'bout witches?" and that nigger was corked up and had to take a back seat. Jim always kept that five-center piece round his neck with a string, and said it was a charm the devil give to him with his own hands, and told him he could cure anybody with it and fetch witches whenever he wanted to just by saying something to it; but he never told what it was he said to it. Niggers would come from all around there and give Jim anything they had, just for a sight of that five-center piece; but they wouldn't touch it, because the devil had had his hands on it. Jim was most ruined for a servant, because he got stuck up on account of having seen the devil and been rode by witches. . . .

In their historical examination of American racial myths which led to institutional racism the authors of this selection state: "Equality and freedom were born on the same soil as slavery and white supremacy."

# 6

# To Serve the Devil

by PAUL JACOBS *and*
SAUL LANDAU

WE SHALL BE as a city upon a hill, John Winthrop told the Puritan settlers of America in 1630. Winthrop assured the men and women who had risked crossing the Atlantic that they had come from the Old to the New World to follow the Lord's bidding,

From "To Serve the Devil," by Paul Jacobs and Saul Landau, in *The Center Magazine*, Volume II, Number 2, March 1969 (Santa Barbara, California: Center for the Study of Democratic Institutions, Fund for the Republic), pp. 40–48. Copyright © 1969 by The Fund for the Republic, Inc. Reprinted by permission of Center for the Study of Democratic Institutions.

to build a Zion in the wilderness, a place from which the light could shine. The Puritans were convinced that only in the New World, unspoiled by European warfare and sin, could a society be built that would be fit for the return of Christ, a country so righteous that God would reward His children by ushering in the Kingdom of the Millennium there. Pious as the first Americans were, however, they could not ignore the wealth that lay before them. The expansion of the frontier was easily fitted into their interpretation of the Lord's will, just as the massacre of Indians and the profitable slave trade had been. American Christianity . . . pre-damned Indians, connived in reducing blacks to chattels, and made a positive virtue of expanding capitalism. . . .

"Providence has been pleased," John Jay wrote in one of the earliest of the *Federalist* papers, "to give this one connected country to one united people —a people descended from the same ancestors, speaking the same language, professing the same religion, attached to the same principles of government, very similar in their manners and customs. . . ." Providence was also on hand to justify the lust for land and wealth owned by Indians, Mexicans, Spaniards, and later, Hawaiians and Eskimos; Providence supported the plantation owners' holding of Negro slaves; Providence vindicated the enforced indenturing of Orientals, the importation of Filipinos and Puerto Ricans as cheap laborers—all of them, after all, were by nature inferior to those whom Providence had blessed with white skin. Might became Divine Right and slavery was countenanced by the Constitution, which provided that a slave would be equal to three-fifths of a man, for voting purposes only.

With this philosophy, the fate of the Negro . . . was to work for the white man; the Indian, who proved to be poor slave material, had to be moved out of the white man's way; the Mexican, if not classed as colored as were Indians and Negroes, was another cultural enemy who held territory that the expanding white man needed. Eventually, even the Hawaiians were "civilized" by having their lands taken from them. . . .

In the struggle for more and more territory, the whites always won—buying it or stealing it—not only because they had more deadly arms but also because Indians, Mexicans, and Hawaiians did not comprehend the white settlers' view of the land or their lust for it. Individual possession and use of the land was not understood by peoples who believed in a mystical relationship between Earth and the Sun and thought that the land was for the use of all. They were willing, as Sitting Bull once said, "to yield to our neighbors, even our animal neighbors, the same right as ourselves to inhabit this land." Such a concept was virtually unknown in the European world. Perhaps only the Quakers understood something of what one Indian chief said to the Governor of Pennsylvania in 1796: "We love quiet; when the woods are rustled by the wind, we fear not; when the leaves are disturbed in ambush, we are uneasy; when a cloud obscures our brilliant sun, our eyes feel dim; but when the rays appear, they give great heat to the body and joy to the heart. Treachery darkens the chain of friendship; but truth makes it brighter than ever. This is the peace we desire."

The majority of the Indians were not to have that peace, any more than the Negroes, Mexicans, Californios, Hawaiians, or any other group that was seen over the centuries as an obstacle to the dynamic expansionism of America. . . .

Foreign observers have found the American experience puzzling. Gunnar Myrdal described it as a dilemma. The nation was the birthplace of modern democracy; and yet it institutionalized racism. Equality and freedom were born on the same soil as slavery and white supremacy. Frontier democracy was itself partly shaped in wars against the Indian and the Mexican: only through collective agreement and political equality could the settlers protect the lands that they had taken. Each white man was entitled to one vote—and a rifle.

Every region of America developed a democratic political system that expanded the franchise to all whites by the eighteen-thirties. The assimilation of European immigrants and the westward movement shaped new and democratic institutions but it also created a frontier racism that joined with the racial hatred to be found in the rising cities and the Southern slave culture. While our history has been glorified as a great outstretching of freedom and democracy, there was from the first a strain of bigotry that has been transmitted to every generation of Americans. Few Americans today, as a consequence, know that such ideas as black power and self-determination, which seem to be heard now for the first time, have deep roots in our national life. Today's ghetto and barrio politics date back to the formation of our segregated—or self-segregated—communities. The ancestors of Malcolm X and Eldridge Cleaver are Nat Turner and Toussaint L'Ouverture. "Reindeer men, get together," the cry of some Eskimos in 1969, should have a familiar resonance. Reies Tijerina, in New Mexico, is only the latest in a long line of Hispano-Indian leaders who organized resistance to whites. From the beginning, the Indians were faced with making a decision forced upon them by the white Europeans hungry for more land: Should they give up the earth on which they lived and the civilizations associated with it, should they resist even at the cost of physical annihilation, or should they try to remain a separate community? The Word plus the Gun forced each subsequent nonwhite group to look to its self-preservation and explore the few possibilities open to it.

One such option, made familiar in the nineteen-sixties under the name of separatist black power, is an integral part of early American history, although it is rarely discussed in that context. The first treaty signed by the newly formed United States was with the Delaware Indian tribe in 1778. It granted the opportunity to the Delawares and "any other tribes who have been friends to the interests of the United States, to join the present confederation, and to form a state, whereof the Delaware nation shall be the head and have a representative in Congress. . . ." Not until early in the twentieth century and the dissolution of the Cherokee nation did Indians formally give up the pursuit of that notion of exercising "red power" through the formation of a separate Indian state with its own representative in Congress.

In 1812, Tecumseh, the Shawnee leader, and Pushmataha, the Choctaw orator, debated fiercely at a Choctaw and Chickasaw council over how best to deal with the white man. "Are we not being stripped, day by day, of the little that remains of our ancient liberty?" Tecumseh asked the council. "Do they not even now kick and strike us as they do their black-faces? How long will it be before they tie us to a post and whip us and make us work for them in cornfields as they do them? Shall we wait for that

Cesar Chavez, a modern Chicano hero, organized the grape workers into their first union, the National Farm Workers Association. (Barbara Fishman Pfeffer)

moment or shall we die fighting before submitting to such ignominy?" Opposing Tecumseh's plea for armed resistance to the whites, Pushmataha implored the tribes to accept the white man's good intentions and urged them to "submit their grievances, whatever they may be, to the Congress of the United States according to the articles of the treaty existing between us and the American people. . . ."

Few Americans know of that history, or know of the heroes of the past in the Southwest and California. Mexicans and Californios, champions of *La Raza,* emerged, usually with pistols in their hands, and often killed the accommodators. . . . They are known, however, to all the young *chicanos* who are today turning to their past. This part of American history lives on only in *corridos* or folk ballads. The debates between different sectors of the conquered Spanish-speaking population remain buried and untranslated in the columns of old newspapers. They, too, had asked: Should we let the white man come in and take our land, or should we organize with guns and fight for our land and our culture? "Long live our country," begins a stanza of a Texas *corrido,* "although suffering setback . . . the mother country is home, that loves son and daughter, for Mexico has fame, military discipline."

The proud Polynesians of the Hawaiian Islands tried resisting the political and cultural white invasion of their shores. "The Hawaiian people will be trodden underfoot by the foreigners," said the people of Lahaina on the island of Maui in 1845. "The laws of those governments will not do for us. Their laws are good for them; our laws are good laws which we have made for ourselves. We are not slaves to serve them. When they talk in their clever way we know what is right and what is wrong. . . ." But it did no good. Very quickly, their country was completely in the control of the *haoles,* the whites with their guns and religion; in a few short decades, the Hawaiians were to become a pitifully small remnant of their race, occupying the lowest rungs in the social and economic ladder of the Islands. The Chinese colony in Hawaii resisted by helping Chinese workers escape from the virtual slave conditions of the white-owned plantations. And at one point, hundreds of Chinese gathered at a mass meeting in Honolulu to "solemnly protest against the injustices, degradation, and insult threatened to be imposed upon us and our race. . . . While we ask for nothing more than equality with other residents of equally good behavior, we shall be satisfied with and shall support and respect nothing that accords to our race a lesser degree of consideration and justice than residents of other nationalities enjoy."

The response of the dominant white community was clear. The Chinese, stated one leading newspaper, "assume an attitude plainly defiant and closely bordering on the dominant and dictatorial. From the weak and lowly field hand of the time of 1851 and the wage scale of three dollars a month, they have, by an unparalleled and alarming evolution, reached the station of an assertive element in the policy of the nation." After that statement was published, the Hawaiian Chinese organized themselves into a protective group and purchased rifles to defend themselves and their homes from the whites.

The Japanese immigrant community in Hawaii knew similar conflicts. Some Japanese sought to resist the brutalities of the white plantation owners by organizing for better conditions. The organizers were jailed and were even attacked by members of their own community who said that "certain things" existed among the Japanese "which cause us to be disliked by American people."

In the years before World War II, the argument within the Japanese community on the mainland echoed the earlier one in Hawaii. Many of the Nisei, the second-generation Japanese, insisted that the only way to demonstrate their patriotism was to become more "American" than the whites, while others insisted on retaining ties with Japan. A third group wanted to resist their treatment as second-class citizens.

Pearl Harbor resolved the argument: "For the sake of internal quiet," according to Franklin D. Roosevelt, all the Japanese, citizens and aliens alike, no matter what attitude they had held, were taken to relocation camps. The debate continued in the camps, accompanied by a great deal of violence, as the "Blood Brothers," a Nisei group determined to fight against the treatment they were receiving, attacked the *inu,* the "dogs," who were willing to accept the relocation process and accommodate to it. Eventually, the government decided to allow the Nisei to serve in the war—against Germany. Of an expected 3550, only twelve hundred Nisei youth volunteered to serve in the segregated "Go for Broke" battalion. Later, when the Nisei were asked to sign a loyalty oath to the United States, nearly half of them refused. After the war ended, some American-born Japanese emigrated to Japan. Ten years later, at least one congressman admitted he had been wrong in his attitude toward the Japanese-Americans: "They were," he said, magnanimously, "just as loyal as those whose skin was white."

White immigrant groups did not escape the bigotry of those who preceded them in America.

Armed with rifle, an Indian protects his nets in defiance
of Washington and Oregon authorities who have banned

commercial fishing above the Bonneville Dam. Indians claim their fishing rights are protected by an 1855 treaty. (Wide World)

Often enough, though, they do not wish to be reminded of that part of their own history. Having achieved some power and status, even if the power is limited and the status uneasy, the assimilated groups join in celebrating America, helping to perpetuate the pervasive myths that have grown up about the character of life in the United States.

Though the melting pot has meant eventual assimilation, it has come only after long years of self-maintained isolation. The Italian or Polish or Jewish workers were given the right to vote on attaining citizenship, but they remained in their ghettos for generations. For them democracy was a fact of life, and although they faced difficult economic struggles they could and did vote and could and did hope that their children would escape the primitive hardships of the first generation. They did not know and perhaps would not care that blacks, Mexicans, and Indians had no hope of participating in the political process. The descendants of these immigrant ethnic and religious groups have even lost track of their own history, which was so often a struggle against racism and religious bigotry. . . .

Most Americans who live outside the ghettos or enclaves knew so little of what is happening inside them that they were surprised and shocked when recent racial conflicts ripped their cities, when anti-Semitism affected an election in New Jersey, when Mexican-Americans became mountain guerrillas in New Mexico, when Indians in the Pacific Northwest went to jail rather than give up their rights to fish.

Americans are surprised and shocked because they live in a mythical country. In this mythical America, the conditions of Negroes, Indians, and Spanish-speaking Americans are assumed to be gradually but inevitably improving as court decisions, governmental efforts, and education break down the barriers of discrimination and prejudice. The injustices and crimes committed by frontier Americans against the Indians are described as regrettable but necessary—or part of another era—and the reservation system, through which the government made wards of the Indians, was an attempt to redress the wrongs. The wholesale theft of land from Mexico through the device of the Mexican War with the resulting degradation of the Spanish-speaking peoples is held to be another lamentable but necessary episode in the country's need to expand. The myth takes in the gradual movement of Negroes toward equality. Negro slavery is acknowledged as a moral wrong, and prejudice against Negroes linked with overt discrimination is, too. In mythical America the country slowly is coming to accept Negroes as equals. The grade-school textbooks say so, and President Johnson put the country on record: "We shall overcome."

Mass media—particularly the movies and television—are the most powerful persuaders or brainwashers of the twentieth century. This selection discusses how the movies have successfully created a stereotypic image of blacks.

# 7

# The Era of Dummies and Darkies

by STEPHEN FAY

IT IS not surprising, though it is certainly significant, that the three best remembered black film stars of the first half of the century are Buckwheat, Farina and Mickey Mouse. While it could hardly be contested that Buckwheat and Farina, those endearing ragamuffins of the "Our Gang" series, were popular black screen personalities, some might challenge the legitimacy of including Walt Disney's renowned rodent in the thin ranks of Negro film stars on the grounds that Mickey (though black) was not human. Indeed he was not human—a characteristic which makes him eminently qualified for membership in any grouping of Negro screen actors, none of whom was human.

From "The Era of Dummies and Darkies," by Stephen Fay, in *Commonweal*, October 30, 1970, pp. 125–28. Copyright © 1970 by Commonweal Publishing Co., Inc. Reprinted by permission of Commonweal Publishing Co., Inc.

There has been, and there still is, an odious trend in the American cinema to avoid depicting the black man as a human being. This "inhuman" tendency has brought about cinematic efforts in which the black man has been portrayed as anything from an imbecile to an Albert Schweitzer, but with painfully few exceptions a living, feasible black human being has not been on the American screen. The treatment of the Negro in American movies has been an incredible, outrageous business. Yet, the sometimes racist, sometimes silly attitude of Hollywood toward the blacks has undergone a fascinating evolution.

The Negro arrived on the American screen in 1910 when Vitagraph Studios released the first film version of Harriet Beecher Stowe's classic of condescending honkyism, *Uncle Tom's Cabin.* The attitude of the movie-makers toward the slump-shouldered, tongue-lolling blacks in this primitive flicker was made clear by the words they used to advertise their wares:

> It will be the real thing in every
> respect—real ice, real bloodhounds,
> real actors and real Negroes!

These innocent and unsophisticated days of calling a spade a spade were short-lived. With the release of D. W. Griffith's *Birth of a Nation* in 1915, a blow was struck for white supremacy with such frankness that future attempts to demonstrate this principle were doomed to be anti-climactic. For one thing, the Ku Klux Klansmen are depicted as severe, but nevertheless just, preservers of the law in the chaotic, antebellum South. The folk-image of the black man as a walking phallus is personified in Gus, an

emancipated slave whose one aim in life is to rape
the ivory-skinned, golden-haired daughter of his former master. He nearly succeeds in getting her between the sheets when the noble band capture Gus
and hang him.

Though the Ku Klux Klan's popularity has di-
minished in most responsible circles, the mythology
about the black man, particularly in regard to his
alleged lust for white flesh, is still accepted as truth
by people who should know better. One such person
is William Styron who perpetuated this bit of
mythological cockamania in his Pulitzer Prize-win-
ning novel, *The Confessions of Nat Turner*. The
portrayal of the black man in *Birth of a Nation* was
not merely libelous; considering the fact that the
"Negroes" in the film were actually white actors
playing blackface, the film comes off as a blatant
fraud.

Still, these early films were experimental and
uncertain. It was not until the early twenties that the
experience and judgment of film-makers crystalized
into a recognizable form: comedy. These were the
films of a more naive era, when audiences could
laugh at the confusion of Willie Best without feeling
guilty, or see something of their grandmothers in
Louise Beavers without consulting their analysts. In
the light-hearted realm of comedy of the twenties
and thirties, one can discern two distinct types of
screen blacks: the Dummies and the Darkies.

Every ethnic group of the screen had its arche-
typal personality back then, i.e., Edgar Kennedy: the
ultimate Irish cop; Richard Loo: the consummate
rat-fink Nip of the war films; Elisha Cook, Jr.: the
supreme squealer. In the black cinema, the arche-
typal Dummy was the marvelous Mantan Moreland.
Don't be too hasty in claiming you've never heard of

Mantan Moreland. Remember that slight, saucer-eyed, shiny-skinned black man who has always played the part of either a night-watchman in a cemetery (into which the Three Stooges invariably stumbled), or the porter in the sleeping car of a train on which Abbot and Costello were traveling. The scenes featuring the Dummy were unfailingly similar: while inspecting the darkest corner of the cemetery, or while sweeping up a dimly-lit corridor of the train in the wee hours, the Dummy would hear a suspicious sound. His eyes would widen to impossible hugeness, his ears perk up and his mouth tightens into a grimace of nameless terror. Then . . . slowly he turns, his features quivering involuntarily, and he finally wheels about to confront . . . Lawd-amercy! a mud-caked Oliver Hardy, or a horribly reddened Huntz Hall who has just emerged from a vat of catsup. The Dummy's reaction to all this? Boinnng! A magnificent double-take, his cap magically leaps from his head, his eyes start from their sockets and he whispers down to his legs which are quivering like so much Jello: "Feets, get goin'!" With a final yelp he races away and dives through a window or races down the road (hurried along by a speeded-up camera) and disappears over the horizon.

Everyone laughed, but it was not with a malicious laughter that audiences regarded the Dummy's antics; it was with the innocently cruel mirth of children. Similar innocence, though one might call it ignorance, was demonstrated by film-makers in their characterization of the second type of black funnymen of the twenties and thirties, the Darkie.

An excellent argument could be made for the case that the single, all-consuming ambition of the screen Darkie was to teach Shirley Temple how to dance.

The ultimate exponent of Darkie-ism was "Bojangles Robinson," whose combination of shuckin' and jivin' humor and light feet would have touched the heart of Stephen Foster.

As mentioned, the Darkie's happier hours were spent with the dimpled child prodigy of the good ship Lollipop. In *Bright Eyes* and *Little Miss Broadway* black butlers taught Shirley the merits of singing a cheerful song when she felt low; in *The Little Colonel* the Negro house-servant tutored her in the joys of tap-dancing up the stairs.

As the years passed, the Darkie reluctantly shuffled off the screen. But he would not be forgotten. He had performed great services for his white masters: in *Birth of the Blues* he taught Bing Crosby how to play the clarinet. His terpsichorean influence on Shirley Temple cannot be over-emphasized. He was more dedicated than Lassie: he even returned from his cinematic grave in the fifties to give Danny Kaye a new lease on life in *The Five Pennies*.

The black man of the screen had to stay at home with the women and children during World War II while John Wayne and Errol Flynn were making the world safe for democracy. As everyone knew, fighting the war was men's work, so the Negro of the films was temporarily out of work. But after Superman had foiled the last, desperate, secret invasion plans of the Nazis, and Dana Andrews and Frederic March had returned from the front, a new black phenomenon appeared on the screen. The Negro of the postwar films was the product of a startling discovery in Hollywood: the word leaked out that the Emancipation Proclamation had been ratified. Further, rumor had it that some blacks (and not just the uppity ones) were a bit discontented with their status in the United States.

For a fleeting moment on the American screen the racially "aware" film came to the fore. Among these gems were *Pinky, Lost Boundaries,* and *Band of Angels.* All of these films, and others of the genre, were disasters. They supposed they could depict the problems and concerns of the Negro in white America, but in so trying they left out one essential detail: the Negroes. In *Pinky* Jeanne Crain played the part of the social-climbing black girl; in *Lost Boundaries* it was Mel Ferrer (talk about ethnic versatility: he portrayed a sulky Jew in *The Sun Also Rises*); in *Band of Angels* Yvonne de Carlo went blackface.

Though the above-mentioned films were box-office flops and generally worthless, the treatment of the American Negro hit the most memorable low with the brief fling movie-makers took at producing black sexploitation films. *I Passed For White,* was the ultimate insult in this area, and it eminently deserved to be awarded a libel suit from the NAACP.

Things were looking pretty grim for the screen Negro of the late fifties. They were losing what little ground they had: the Three Stooges had a corner on the Dummy market; Gene Kelly could dance circles around the docile Darkie; and there was no way on earth movie-makers could return the Negro to the cinematic cotton fields and watermelon patches. Hope was finally found in the massive frame of folklore's epitome of black power, John Henry.

A score of films were released in the late fifties and early sixties in which (somewhere in the lower ranks of the cast) a muscular, taciturn black man could be found. The feature spot for the John Henry in these movies always involved some incredible feat of strength or physical prowess. In *The Devil At Four O'Clock* he hefted a sagging bridge which was about to tumble into a gorge so that the less powerful white people could scurry across. Then he died. In *The Dirty Dozen* he did in most of the Nazi general staff to save his white comrades. Then he died. In *Dark of the Sun* he wiped out a nest of feisty cut-throats and rescued his white co-star from certain doom. Then he died.

The John Henry genre was a popular one, but it, unfortunately, died out (literally).

*And Then . . .*

Like the Tin Woodsman and Scarecrow of *The Wizard of Oz,* the black man of filmdom longed for a heart and a mind. A new image was needed. As civil rights legislation passed in Congress, so too was equality demanded for the Negro of the screen. The film world responded to this urging with a singular lack of temperance and judgment, creating the most astonishing, breath-taking screen phenomenon since the day Colin Clive unveiled the first Frankenstein monster: Sidney Poitier, alias Super Spade.

A Super Spade is a perfectly incredible amalgam of the best parts of Socrates, Abe Lincoln, Popeye, Sherlock Holmes and Jesus. His overwhelming virtue is not that he possesses more zip and joy than Rootie Kazootie, nor even that he is more wise and perceptive than the Shadow; everyone loves Super Spade because he is not too black. His features are not too Negroid, his skin is not too dark.

A Super Spade performs more miraculous missions of mercy in a single day than any white man could effect in twenty years. In one of the first films of this genre, *Lilies of the Field,* Poitier rescues a band of needy nuns from financial disaster, assists an impoverished padre in his struggle against demon rum, single-handedly constructs a chapel out of sticks

Sidney Poitier starred as a suave black doctor in *Guess Who's Coming to Dinner.* (Culver Pictures, Inc.)

and cow dung, then quietly slips off, leaving the grateful objects of his benevolence wondering (as did the Lone Ranger's beneficiaries): "Who was that man?"

In *To Sir With Love* Super Spade transforms a wretched classroom of greasy pachucos and aspiring whores into young ladies and gentlemen of refinement. By his good example alone he revamps the entire British educational system. He further demonstrated, in his spare time, that he could box like Joe Palooka, dance like Rudolph Nureyev, and cook like Julia Child.

Super Spade hits his peak in *Guess Who's Coming to Dinner*. In this abominable effort he is not only dashing, handsome, sexy and articulate—he is the greatest doctor in the history of medicine. He has garnered more awards and Nobel Prizes than you could fit into Fibber McGee's closet.

Superlatives cannot do justice to Super Spade, much as film-makers can seemingly do no justice to the black man. Arguments to the contrary become untenable in light of the most recent addition to the continuing adventures of Super Spade, *The Lost Man*. In this timely delight Sidney Poitier portrays a black militant (about as successfully as Knucklehead Smiff could portray William F. Buckley). In fact, to our great relief, Sidney turns out to be a Robin Hood of the ghettos, not really black, not really a militant.

More recent films are sufficiently dismal to warrant my belief that these movies are crummy and due to get crummier. *Putney Swope* (which came out last summer) billed itself as something different. In fact, it is in the billing itself that one may find a grand insight as to just how "different" *Putney Swope* is. The newspaper and theater ads for *Putney Swope* featured a black hand earnestly flipping the bird. And though the film had some really funny bits, it was essentially comprised of vengeful vignettes in which blacks flipped the metaphorical bird to whitey. The black man is shown beating white America at its own games, but who cares? Why should blacks want to play at white man's games? This whole effort, which reaches a horrid low with the Black Miss America Contest, is a drag and a waste of time. . . .

Thus, under the banner of up from knavery the black man of films has evolved. Though in 1935 Charles Bickford could kick his black coolie in the teeth with his hobnail boots in *The Plainsman,* the 1968 remake of that film would tolerate no such cruelty. The black man has been awarded a mind and a heart (though both of these "advances" have been made with unpalatable clumsiness). Yet the Negro of the American films has always been, and still is, a fraud, a joke, or an insult. After sixty years of trial and error (and mostly error) the black man depicted on the screen remains unreal and consistently comes up lacking. What does he lack? Need we ask? He got no *soul.*

And herein lies a possible resolution to half a century of foolishness. What is needed in the film world is segregation. A recent ray of hope, entitled *Nothing But A Man,* endorses this suggestion, as it was made entirely by a black film staff. For who but a Negro can portray a Negro, and who should coach him but a black man, and who should mobilize him but a black screen-writer? Will this emerging trend last? Will this one bit of rationality and sanity survive, or will the executives of Hollywood continue to serve a more aware audience the same vapid plate of warmed-over blackface?

In Puerto Rico the color of one's skin is of slight importance, but when a Puerto Rican comes to the mainland he becomes acutely aware of the predominant American attitude toward color. Thus, he soon learns that white is an important asset to improving one's status and that nonwhite is a stigma. The following first-person account of episodes in the life of a Puerto Rican reveals his experiences with racism.

# 8

# A Puerto Rican in New York and Other Sketches

by JESÚS COLÓN

*Hiawatha into Spanish*

THE OLD *New York World* was a great paper. I bought it mainly for the Heywood Broun column "It Seems To Me," and for the pages and pages of

From *A Puerto Rican in New York and Other Sketches*, by Jesús Colón (New York: Mainstream Publishers, Inc., 1961), pp. 49–51, 118. Copyright © 1961 by Mainstream Publishers, Inc. Reprinted by permission of New Outlook Publishers & Distributors, Inc.

A Puerto Rican arriving in New York with hope for a better life. . . . (Barbara Fishman Pfeffer)

Help Wanted ads. I got many a "good" porter job through these Help Wanted pages of the *New York World*. Once, I also got myself a job as a translator from these same pages.

Those were the days of the silent films. A film agency somewhere in the Times Square area was asking for a person who could translate the explanatory material like "One Year Later" into Spanish, so that the films could be used in Latin America. Half a penny a word was to be paid. The translator was to work in his own home and all transactions were to be done through the mail. The agency gave a post office box number to which you were supposed to write.

I wrote. The agency mailed me the material to be translated for one short film. I returned the completed translation. Then they sent me a small check, and more work. It seems that they were satisfied.

Time passed. My old Oliver typewriting machine continued to grind translations of inspirational thoughts such as: "The morning after," "One week after," "Five years after." Sometimes a description or historical paragraph such as an introduction to a striking panorama or a scene helped to break the monotony of the hackneyed phrase and the routine short dialogue.

During the early twenties, the episode or chapter of a serial was a standard feature accompanying the main picture in a movie house. At the end of the episode the hero or more often the heroine was left hanging by two fingers from the edge of a cliff or surrounded by half a dozen lions in the middle of an African jungle. The idea was to excite enough curiosity for you to return next week to see what surely appeared, from all logical deduction, like certain death for the hero or heroine. But—what do you know! She or he was miraculously saved from a horrible ending by one of the thousand props that the director always had ready to extract from his shirt sleeve and the serial went on and on for months. Today, you can only see these serials chapter by chapter every week in the cheapest of the movie houses or on the most idiotic of the TV programs.

To me, these serials were a gold mine. I was the first to wish the hero eternal life—the longer the serials, the more money I could earn.

One morning I received a long poem that was supposed to be the life of a young American Indian. It was to be used in one of those nature pictures full of rushing rivers, whispering pine trees, bounding deer and flocks of birds suddenly rising out of the thick foliage frightened by the unexpected appearance of "man." The poem was long. The name of the poem was "Hiawatha" by Henry Wadsworth Longfellow. Well, at last I got something worth translating! For a few days I concentrated on making a comparative study of the English and Spanish meter, poetic accent, rhyme and rhythm, before I actually tackled the task of translating the poem itself. It was work. It was fun. Some additional explanation in prose helped in giving clarity and unity to the many natural scenes in the film. The poem itself was broken into sections and these were inserted among the panoramic sequences. When I finished the translation I felt I had done a good job of it.

Hiawatha was sent to the film agency. A few days later I received a complimentary letter with a check. The letter also invited me to come to the office on a certain date. I was being offered steady employment at the agency at a weekly salary.

I got up very early the day of the appointment. I

took a great deal of time washing, dressing and combing my hair so that I would look my best. I wore my Sunday suit. The office took up about half an entire floor, way up in a tall building. I asked for the man who had signed the letter. Yes, he was in.

The minute I told him who I was and showed him the letter he himself had signed offering me steady work as a translator, he assumed a cold and impersonal attitude. He made it short and to the point. "Yes, I wrote that letter. I invited you to come to translate for us here at the office." And, pointing to the other side of the room, he added, "That was to be your desk and typewriter. But I thought you were white."

Then and there that day in the early twenties, I added one more episode to the maturing serial of my life.

### Greetings from Washington

. . . One time I went to Washington. I don't remember on what delegation or committee. It would take us at least two days to finish our business in the Capital. So I took every precaution to see that I had a place to sleep at least for a night. A friend gave me a letter to a Negro family in Washington. They would have space for me to sleep for one night. The delegation went to the various offices we had to go to. After a good day's legwork from building to building we went into one of the government cafeterias—one of the few places where Negroes and whites can eat together unmolested—in downtown Washington—and had our supper. We agreed on a place in which we were to meet next morning and everybody left for the house in which a nice soft bed was waiting for him. Or so I thought.

I went to the Negro family's address to whom our mutual friend in New York had given me a very nice letter of introduction. I knocked on the door and waited. After a while, I knocked again. Then again and more persistently and strongly. A neighbor in the next apartment opened the door. "Are you looking for Mr. and Mrs.——?" "Yes." "They went to New York for a few days to visit their folks in Jamaica, Long Island."

"What shall I do now?" I thought to myself. It was already around 8:30 or 9:00 o'clock in the evening. I had a little over twenty dollars in my wallet. I went to the railroad station and returned the little overnight valise to one of the boxes in which, for twenty-five cents, you could lock anything from a briefcase to a suitcase. I wanted to be free to walk and move around without any extra weight bothering me. Then I started to look for a place to sleep.

I visited half a dozen hotels, large and medium size. They all said the same thing: No colored people allowed. When I went to three or four rather dilapidated and suspicious looking rooming houses offering any price they asked for a cot somewhere in which to pass the night, I met with the same answer: "No colored allowed."

Suddenly I remembered that a Jewish friend had given me the telephone number of a girl friend of his who worked for the government in Washington. I had it written on the margin of my *New York Times* that I had in the valise and that I had no time to read during the day. I went back to the railroad station to get the valise and the address.

By now it was eleven o'clock at night. I called the number, gave my friend's name in New York, as an introduction. Then I explained my situation. Ev-

Some of the burdens of the nonwhite citizen.   (Ed Lettau)

erything. She told me to come but not to take the elevator. She explained that she lived in an apartment building for whites only. If anybody knew that she was inviting a Negro to sleep at her place, she would be sure to lose her apartment— So she gave me her apartment number and detailed instructions on how to avoid being seen coming in by anybody. I will remember that night all my life. I went into that apartment building as if I were actually going to commit a crime. Avoiding everybody, walking on tiptoes as silently and stealthily as possible! And to think that I was going to do what millions of people were doing in over half the world at that very hour: Going to sleep! But in Washington the "Capital of the world's greatest democracy," I had to act like a thief just to get a place where I could go to bed and fall asleep!

The young lady shared the apartment with another office worker friend of hers. I slept on a sofa in the parlor. It was agreed that I would get up very early so that I could leave as unseen as I came in the night before. This I did. All this happened a few years ago. If you place the two young ladies—they must be older now—right in front of me today, I confess that I would not recognize them. All I know is that both of them were waiting for my knock, dressed in their housecoats, when I came into their apartment. Wherever you are ladies, from these pages of reminiscences, thank you again. . . .

I remember the time that Ava Miranda and some of her friends went from Brooklyn to visit their uncle in Washington. Some of the girls were white and some were Negroes. Their uncle, a Puerto Rican veteran of the First World War, had lived in Washington for many years. He was supposed to be a "small" big shot in Washington. A Puerto Rican who felt himself to be 200 per cent American, who on Armistice Day was the first to be in line with his 1917 uniform, ribbons, and medals, ready to parade down Pennsylvania Avenue and show the world the equality, freedom and liberty you could find in Washington, Capital of the U.S.A. He was the kind who believed in everything that the books said—and then more. He was a Puerto Rican who had gradually and unconsciously converted himself into a flag waving, pledge taking, bigger and better 200 per cent American.

As soon as the girls left the New York train, uncle took them to the first restaurant in sight. The restaurant owner insisted he would serve the white girls but not the Negro girls. Uncle was very much incensed. He felt it was his obligation to prove to the young ladies that there was equality and democracy in Washington. "I am a veteran of the First World War. Remember THAT!" he used to shout when somebody dared to doubt that he would be able to do anything about it. When they were not served at the restaurant, uncle went to the Police Department. He went to the higher authorities. There he was courteously laughed at. He made dozens of telephone calls and kept writing dozens of letters long after the young ladies returned to New York. Yes, sir, he wanted to prove to the girls that there was such a thing as equality and democracy in Washington. I heard uncle died without even being able to win an apology from the restaurant owners. . . .

The selection that follows is a discussion among four young Mexican-Americans about racism in the United States as they have experienced it living in an East Los Angeles slum. "Our people have been saying brown power for hundreds of years—only we've been saying it in Spanish," says one of the youths.

# 9

## La Junta

by STAN STEINER

IT IS a long, hot summer afternoon. Four young men from the poorest barrios of East Los Angeles lounge about beneath the lazy palm trees. In the suburban house of shabby elegance, mocked by once-gracious lawns and broken garden-urns, the young men of the streets eat cheese sandwiches and drink beer and

From "La Junta" in *La Raza*, by Stan Steiner (New York: Harper and Row, Publishers, 1970), pp. 113–17. Reprinted by permission of Harper & Row, Publishers, Inc., and Harold Matson Company, Inc.

Chicano children—lost between two cultures. (Barbara Fishman Pfeffer)

philosophize about bygone Aztec kingdoms and utopias of brown power and poetry they have liked and the police who have beaten them up. Summer days inspire dreams. And these "young toughs," as the police call them, are romantic and wistful.

Who are these young dreamers? They are the Chicanos of La Junta.

All summer the Los Angeles Police Department has feared trouble in the barrio from these youths. "The *placas* [police] have treated us like *'pendejos'* [literally, 'pubic hairs']," the Chicanos say, "because they do not understand us." These young men are rebels, but are philosophical about their rebellion.

José: "If you have a rebellion you have to have

something to rebel against. So you may become racist. Stone racist. Is 'brown power' racist? No, 'brown power' is cultural. So it doesn't have to become racist."

Hector: "I wonder. Why do militants create a lot of alienation in their communities?"

José: "Man, we're not rebelling. We're building something. We're trying to create less alienation and more community unity. A man without knowledge of his people is like a tree without a root. What we're trying to do is get people this cultural consciousness. Brown power is to know your culture."

Roberto: "I agree with him. Brown power has to be different from black power because we are not black."

Hector: "I don't agree with that. You ask a black man, What is black power? He's going to tell you, well, black power is like the black man being able to take over his institutions, running his own thing. It's black institutions run by black people for the betterment of black people. That's what he'll tell you. You know, basically, we want that."

José: "I think we have to go farther than that! Brown power has to be our cultural heritage. So we can get those values that were inherent in the Indians of ancient Mexico. And we can take those same values and same culture and use it in our lives and our movement. The way an Indian would relate to his family, to his tribe; the pride he had in his Indian nation. Brown power is first of all nationalism. But it isn't nationalism that we have to learn from reading what some intellectual says, like black people do. This is nationalism that we know existed among our people thousands of years ago. It was true then, today, and it will be true a hundred years from now."

Hector: "Our people have been saying brown power for hundreds of years—only we have been saying it in Spanish."

Chuck: "Like before anything ever started, we used to get together, some dudes where I live at, we used to drink and all that, and we used to be talking—before black power, before they had the riots and everything. Viva La Raza! and Chicano power! and Brown Power!—about things like that. So if you ask how come we copy the black people? It's just we didn't come on until later on. We didn't do all kinds of demonstrations. But we always had it. We always said it. Among ourselves."

Once these young men were Brown Berets and wore the defiant caps with the insignia of the Holy Cross and two crossed rifles. "The brown beret was chosen because it is a symbol of the love and pride we have in our race, and in the color of our skin," the manifesto of the youth group declares. A barrio "Self-Defense" unit in the beginning, it was established "to keep a watchful eye" on the police and to protect the rights of Chicano youth "by all means necessary."

In their pockets the Brown Berets carry "calling cards" with the motto "To Serve, Observe, Protect," and the message at the bottom, "You Have Just Been Helped By," with space for the bearer's name. Newspapers have compared the Brown Berets to "a Mexican imitation of the Black Panthers." In a national magazine the youth group was described as a "highly disciplined" and "paramilitary organization." "We have information that they are receiving semimilitary training," an intelligence officer of the Los Angeles Sheriff's Department was quoted as saying. He talked of "bayonet drills." One latter-day dime novel forecast a "Brown Beret Revolution,"

with the fearful words, "the revolution is on," because the manifesto of the Brown Berets asserts their
right to bear arms: "We demand the right to keep
and bear arms to defend our communities against
racist police as guaranteed under the Second Amend-
ment of the United States Constitution."

These young men have left the Brown Berets. "It
is not enough to rebel," one says. They are search-
ing for something more lasting, to build something
new.

Roberto: "I don't really know what brown power
is. To me it's a new feeling I have."

Hector: "Brown power means liberation to me.
I don't want to be outnumbered by Anglos ten to
one. I don't want to conform to what they want.
Some little old lady in Pasadena is figuring out right
now what us wetbacks will be doing next week.
What freeway is going to run through my home. I
don't go for that. I want to determine what is right
for me."

Roberto: "It's not a racial thing."

José: "You see, we have some black Mexicans.
We have some Mexicans with blue eyes and blond
hair and white skin. He's a surfer, you would think.
He's not. He's a Mexican. He can take it any way
he wants. The blacks can't do that because their
color is so obvious no matter what they do. What
I'm saying is that brown power is not a black power
sort of thing. Even though we are in the same con-
dition, like brothers, we are not the same. I mean
this is *our* motherland."

Hector: "You are using the white people's words.
English, you see. English is a racist language. That's
why they sound the same—brown power, black
power. In Spanish we don't say a color. We say, the
power of the people—La Raza."

José: "I grew up in San Diego. Well, I used to think I was a good citizen. They say, you be a good citizen and you help your Uncle Sam. So I volunteered. I wanted to be the best, so I volunteered for the paratroopers."

Hector: "Man, he asked what brown power is and you're talking about the paratroopers."

José: "Brown power! That's me!"

In his boyhood José was a paratrooper in Vietnam. He became the "Field Marshal" and elder statesman of the Brown Berets; a thoughtful, toughly philosophical young man of poetic words and a fragile sadness. Hector, with his perpetual dark glasses, talks tougher. He is preparing for college, training himself in intellectual self-defense. Carlos, called Chuck, is sullen and silent. When he talks his thoughts are flat and matter-of-fact, and he does not give himself away. Roberto, the youngest, talks the toughest, but he has a cherubic eye and he shyly whispers that he is a poet. (The poet laureate of the La Junta!)

"Man, don't mention our names," says the former "Field Marshal" José. He feels that the Los Angeles Police Department is trying to harass and arrest the Brown Berets and to destroy their group. The young men agree; no real names.

José: "I'm nervous. Man, I don't know what I'm saying. The thing is I wanted to be a good citizen. Later on after I finished trade school I found out there's something wrong with me. I'm brown! So I started saying, the devil with these people. I'm brown, fine! I don't melt into this big pot, this melting pot *you* call 'America.' You know, oil and water don't mix. So I *have* to float to the top, where I came from, to the top of the pot."

Hector: "We're not in the melting pot sort of thing. Chicanos don't melt."

José: "In this country it's real hard. If you want decent bread you got to go to college. So you get a job for the government. So I have this poor Chicano in front of me and I have to send him to jail for stealing. Hell, the white man stole this whole continent, but white people never think of that. Did the white man ever get punished? No! He got rich. But my duty as a good citizen is to nail my brother! My brother! Why my brother?"

Hector: "There's a lot of Mexicans that are identifying with the Anglo. But the Anglo don't really accept them. In most cases they look down on them too."

Roberto: "So we are like the man with a sword in his chest and nowhere to step back. We are pinned against the wall. . . ."

Hector says, "I don't know what's wrong with white people."

José replies, "Man, the name of the game is racism. The white man is a racist. It's a colorful country."

Hector: "If people are racist, then something made them racist. So we get into the thing: why do we have racism? Mostly everybody says it's economics. Who brought the slaves here? In Mexico they enslaved the Indians purely for economic reasons, to get gold out of the mines. It's greediness that created racism."

José: "If you figure out how the West was won, it was just that. Racism is the democratic tradition."

Hector: "In my mind, this country was built on violence, built on blood. Like the way it's being done in Vietnam, it's the same thing that's always been done here to the people—black or brown. As a matter of fact, wasn't the Cuban revolution fought against the same owners of the same farms that now we're fighting in the San Joaquin Valley?"

José: "You say, Why is the world turning bad on me? The world is sick and tired of being good citizens. The world wants to eat, that's all."

Hector: "Sure. I believe there will be armed conflict in this country between the races."

José: "There's going to be armed conflict. But we won't start nothing like that. We would be wiped out. We ain't that crazy, man."

Vine Deloria, Jr., a Standing Rock Sioux, discusses the racial myths that have split America and analyzes the effect of the black man's revolt upon the Indians. The author offers separatism as a way to solve the racist problems. He says: "Separate but equal has become a battle cry of the black activists. . . . Is it the cry of a dying amalgam of European immigrants who are plagued by the European past? Or is it the lusty cry of a new culture impatient to be born?"

# 10

# The Red
# and the Black

by VINE DELORIA, JR.

CIVIL RIGHTS has been the most important and least understood movement of our generation. To some it has seemed to be a simple matter of fulfilling rights outlined by the Constitutional amendments after the Civil War. To others, particularly church people, Civil Rights has appeared to be a fulfillment of the brotherhood of man and the determination of humanity's relationship to God. To those opposing the

From Chapter 8, *Custer Died For Your Sins, An Indian Manifesto*, by Vine Deloria, Jr. (New York/London: The Mac-Millan Co., 1969), pp. 168, 169, 188, 189, 193, 194. Copyright © 1969 by Vine Deloria, Jr. Reprinted by permission of The MacMillan Company.

movement, Civil Rights has been a foreign conspiracy which has threatened the fabric of our society.

For many years the movement to give the black people rights equal to those of their white neighbors was called Race Relations. The preoccupation with race obscured the real issues that were developing and meant that programs devised to explore the area of race always had a black orientation.

To the Indian people it has seemed quite unfair that churches and government agencies concentrated their efforts primarily on the blacks. By defining the problem as one of race and making race refer solely to black, Indians were systematically excluded from consideration. National church groups have particularly used race as a means of exploring minority-group relations. Whatever programs or policies outlined from national churches to their affiliates and parishes were generally black-oriented programs which had been adapted to include Indians.

There was probably a historical basis for this type of thinking. In many states in the last century, Indians were classified as white by laws passed to exclude blacks. So there was a connotation that Indians might in some way be like whites. But in other areas, particularly marriage laws, Indians were classified as blacks and this connotation really determined the role into which the white man forced the red man. Consequently, as far as most Race Relations were concerned, Indians were classified as nonwhites.

There has been no way to positively determine in which category Indians belong when it comes to federal agencies. The Bureau of Indian Affairs consistently defined Indians as good guys who have too much dignity to demonstrate, hoping to keep the Indian people separate from the ongoing Civil Rights movement. Other agencies generally adopted a semi-black orientation. . . .

The Civil Rights Commission and the Community Relations Service always gave only lip service to Indians until it was necessary for them to write an annual report. At that time they always sought out some means of including Indians as a group with which they had worked the previous fiscal year. That was the extent of Indian relationship with the agency: a paragraph in the annual report and a promise to do something next year.

Older Indians, as a rule, have been content to play the passive role outlined for them by the

A typical racist advertisement contributing to the debasement of the Indian.

bureau. They have wanted to avoid the rejection and bad publicity given activists.

*White culture* destroys other culture because of its abstractness. As a destroyer of culture it is not a culture but a cancer. In order to keep the country from complete divisiveness, separatism must be accepted as a means to achieve equality of personality both for groups and individuals. Separatism can be the means by which blacks gain time for reflection, meditation, and eventual understanding of themselves as a people.

The black needs time to develop his roots, to create his sacred places, to understand the mystery of himself and his history, to understand his own purpose. These things the Indian has and is able to maintain through his tribal life. The Indian now needs to create techniques to provide the economic strength needed to guarantee the survival of what he has.

In a real way, white culture, if there is such, is already doomed to its own destruction. Continual emphasis on racial rather than cultural problems will not only bring down white society but may also endanger ancient Indian society and newly emerging black and Mexican social movements.

The white man has the marvelous ability to conceptualize. He has also the marvelous inability to distinguish between sacred and profane. He therefore arbitrarily conceptualizes all things and understands none of them. His science creates gimmicks for his use. Little effort is made to relate the gimmicks to the nature of life or to see them in a historical context.

The white man is problem-solving. His conceptualizations merge into science and then emerge in his social life as problems, the solutions of which are the adjustments of his social machine. Slavery, prohibition, Civil Rights, and social services are all important adjustments of the white man's social machine. No solution he has reached has proven adequate. Indeed, it has often proven demonic.

White solutions fail because *white* itself is an abstraction of an attitude of mind, not a racial or group reality. The white as we know him in America is an amalgam of European immigrants, not a racial phenomenon. But the temptation has always been present to define groups according to their most superficial aspect. Hence we have white, black, red, and the Yellow Peril. And we are taught to speak of the *Negro problem,* the *Indian problem,* and so forth.

White has been abstracted into a magical nebulous mythology that dominates all inhabitants of our country in their attitudes toward one another. We are, consequently, all prisoners of that mythology so far as we rebel against it. It is our misfortune that our economic system reflects uncritical acceptance of the mythology and that economic movements tend to reinforce the myth. . . .

Winds of caution have set in and sails are being trimmed. There appears to be no means by which the cultural crisis can be understood by those outside the group. Indian people are becoming more and more reluctant to consider alternatives. They are becoming distrustful of people who talk equality because they do not see how equality can be achieved without cultural separateness. To the degree that other groups demand material ransoms for peace and order, Indian people are fearful of the ultimate goals of the different movements.

There is no basic antagonism between black and red, or even between red and white. Conflicts are

Actress Jane Fonda discusses her treatment by military authorities at Fort Lawton, which she and 160 Indians visited in hopes of setting up an Indian cultural center. (UPI)

created when Indians feel they are being defined out of existence by the other groups. Historically, each group has its own road to travel. All roads lead to personal and group affirmation. But the obstacles faced by each group are different and call for different solutions and techniques.

While it is wrong and harmful to define all dark-skinned people by certain criteria, it is also wrong to pretend that they have nothing in common. It is what Indians, blacks, and Mexicans have in common and where their differences lie which should be carefully studied.

Time and again blacks have told me how lucky they were not to have been placed on reservations after the Civil War. I don't think they were lucky at all. I think it was absolute disaster that blacks were not given reservations.

Indian tribes have been able to deal directly with the federal government because they had a recognized status within the Constitutional scheme. Leadership falls into legal patterns on each reservation through the elective process. A tribal chairman is recognized by federal agencies, Congressional committees, and private agencies as the representative of the group. Quarrels over programs, rivalry between leaders, defense of rights, and expressions of the mood of the people are all channeled through the official governing body. Indian people have the opportunity to deal officially with the rest of the world as a corporate body.

The blacks, on the other hand, are not defined with their own community. Leadership too often depends upon newspaper coverage. Black communities do not receive the deference tribes receive, because they are agencies in the private arena and not quasi-governmental. Law and order is something imposed brutally from without, not a housekeeping function of the group.

Above all, Indian people have the possibility of total withdrawal from American society because of their special legal status. They can, when necessary, return to a recognized homeland where time is static and the world becomes a psychic unity again.

To survive, blacks must have a homeland where they can withdraw, drop the facade of integration, and be themselves. Whites are inevitably torn because they have no roots, they do not understand the past, and they have already mortgaged their future. Unless they can renew their psychic selves and achieve a sense of historical participation as a people they will be unable to survive. . . .

On September 10, 1874, this editorial
was published in the **Atlanta News** to
express how southern white Suprema-
cists felt when they were attempting to
regain their prewar positions in their
states. In 1970 there still exist advo-
cates of white supremacy who are form-
ing white leagues to resist, with brute
force if necessary, the enforcement of
the Civil Rights Act as required by law.

# 11

# Meet Brute Force
# with Brute Force

by *Atlanta News*

LET THERE BE White Leagues formed in every
town, village and hamlet of the South, and let us
organize for the great struggle which seems inevitable. If the October elections which are to be held
at the North are favorable to the radicals, the time
will have arrived for us to prepare for the very

From *Great Issues in American History*, Vol. 2: 1864–1954,
edited by Richard Hofstadter (New York: Vintage Books, Alfred
A. Knopf, Inc., 1958), pp. 43–44.

Officials of the Ku Klux Klan, an organization which, even today, is dedicated to keeping the white race in power in America. (UPI)

worst. The radicalism of the republican party must be met by the radicalism of white men. We have no war to make against the United States Government, but against the republican party our hate must be unquenchable, our war interminable and merciless. Fast fleeting away is the day of wordy protests and idle appeals to the magnanimity of the republican party. By brute force they are endeavoring to force us into acquiescence to their hideous programme. We have submitted long enough to indignities, and it is time to meet brute force with brute force. Every Southern State should swarm with White Leagues, and we should stand ready to act the moment Grant signs the civil-rights bill. It will not do to wait till radicalism has fettered us to the car of social equality before we make an effort to resist it. The signing of the bill will be a declaration of war against the southern whites. It is our duty to ourselves, it is our duty to our children, it is our duty to the white race whose prowess subdued the wilderness of this continent, whose civilization filled it with cities and towns and villages, whose mind gave it power and grandeur, and whose labor imparted to it prosperity, and whose love made peace and happiness dwell within its homes, to take the gage of battle the moment it is thrown down. If the white democrats of the North are men, they will not stand idly by and see us borne down by northern radicals and half-barbarous negroes. But no matter what they may do, it is time for us to organize. We have been temporizing long enough. Let northern radicals understand that military supervision of southern elections and the civil-rights bill mean war, and that war means bloodshed, and that we are terribly in earnest, and even they, fanatical as they are, may retrace their steps before it is too late.

In 1964–1965 in Boston, Jonathan Kozol taught a segregated fourth grade class in a corner of an auditorium in which other classes met. He was fired for using a poem by Langston Hughes that was not part of the approved reading designed for black children. In the selection below, he writes about the types of books which have been and are still being used in our school system.

## 12

## Death at an Early Age

by JONATHAN KOZOL

THE AMOUNT of difficulty involved in telling children they are Negro, of course, is proportional to the degree of ugliness which is attached to that word within a person's mind. . . . Why would a teacher fear it? Would it be a thing of which to be afraid? Would it be to tell them something shameful? Would

From *Death at an Early Age* by Jonathan Kozol (Boston: Houghton Mifflin Co.). Copyright © 1967 by Jonathan Kozol. Reprinted by permission of Houghton Mifflin Company and Penguin Books, Ltd., London.

it be equivalent to telling them that they were bad—
or hateful? They were Negro. To be taught by a
teacher who felt that it would be wrong to let them
know it must have left a silent and deeply working
scar. The extension to children of the fears and
evasions of a teacher is probably not very uncom-
mon, and at times the harm it does is probably
trivial. But when it comes to a matter of denying
to a class of children the color of their skin and of
the very word that designates them, then I think that
it takes on the proportions of a madness.

In time, at school, we finished our journey across
America. Next we were to go for an imaginary trip
across the sea. We were to study about the Arabs
and, before we had really begun, the Reading
Teacher came in . . . and urged upon me a book
which she said that she had used with the children
in her own classes for a great many years. From
this book she asked me to pick out a good section
to read. It was not the same geography book that
the children had at their desks. She told me that
she considered it a better one, but that it was too
old to be in regular use. We were studying the
desert. The night before, I looked into the book, and
I found some remarkable writing. It is fortunate that
I looked carefully and made myself some warning
marks before I just walked into the class and started
to read. These are some of the things I found as I
looked through this book:

"The streets of this Oasis city of Biskra are interesting. There are many different people upon
them. Some who are white like ourselves have
come here from Europe. Others are Negroes with
black skins, from other parts of Africa. And many
are bronze-faced Arabs who have come in from the
desert to trade in the stores . . ."

Black girl—white doll.  (Dennis McGuire)

There next is a description of an Arab family: "We meet Ali and Selma and their family near the market place. The Bedouin father is tall and straight. He wears a robe that falls to his ankles, and his bare feet are shod in sandals of camel's leather . . . Behind the Bedouin father walk his wife and his children, Ali and Selma. The Bedouin mother is dressed in a long robe. She, too, wears a cloth over her head to protect it from the sun. Ali and Selma wear clothing like that of their father and mother. Their brown feet are bare and covered with dust.

"These people are fine looking. Their black eyes are bright and intelligent. Their features are much like our own, and although their skin is brown, they belong to the white race, as we do. It is the scorching desert sun that has tanned the skin of the Arabs to such a dark brown color."

After I read this, I was curious to see how the authors would treat the African Negroes. I looked ahead until I found these words:

"The black people who live on this great continent of Africa were afraid of the first white men who came to explore their land. They ran and hid from them in the dark jungle. They shot poisoned arrows from behind the thick bushes. They were savage and uncivilized."

The more I read, the more I thought I could understand why those African people may well have had good reason to be afraid of the first white men: "Yumbu and Minko are a black boy and a black girl who live in this jungle village. Their skins are of so dark a brown color that they look almost black. Their noses are large and flat. Their lips are thick. Their eyes are black and shining, and their hair is so curly that it seems like wool. THEY ARE NEGROES AND THEY BELONG TO THE BLACK RACE."

Turning the pages to a section about Europe, I read by contrast the following description of a very different, and presumably more attractive, kind of child: "Two Swiss children live in a farmhouse on the edge of town . . . These children are handsome. Their eyes are blue. Their hair is golden yellow. Their white skins are clear, and their cheeks are as red as ripe, red apples."

What I felt about the words that I have capitalized above was not that they were wrong, or that there could conceivably ever be anything wrong about saying of a group of people that they are members of a particular race, but simply that the context and the near-belligerence of the assertion make it *sound* degrading. It is not in the facts. It is only in the style. I capitalized those lines, but they feel capitalized when you read them. They are arbitrary in their finality and the feeling they convey is one of categorical and, somehow, almost syntactical ill-fate. It is from reading a book like this over the course of twenty years that the Reading Teacher and thousands of other teachers like her might well come to believe that you would do a child nothing but a disservice to let him know that he was Negro. The books are not issued any more—but the teachers still are. It seems to me that until something has been done to affect those teachers, and to alter the attitudes with which they approach the children in their charge, then none of the other changes are going to make a very great difference, and the overall atmosphere is likely to remain the same.

Accompanying the text about the Congo in this book there were some gory illustrations: half-naked Africans in what are sometimes called characteristic poses, beating on drums and puckering out their mouths and looking truly strange. There was a pho-

tograph of the Pygmies which seemed to make fun
of them and, if it is possible, to "shrink" them and
make them look even littler than they really are. A
straight and handsome tall white hunter is seen
surrounded by tiny, swarming naked people. Their
bellies look bloated and a number of them are grip-
ping arrows or spears. We read these words:

"The most interesting of all the tribes we see
upon the Congo are the tiny Pygmies. The full-grown
men and women of the Pygmy tribes do not weigh
more than a seven-year-old American child. Their
children look like little brown dolls. These Pygmies
are Negroes."

There are few uses in this chapter of such words
as "skillful," "well-developed," "pride," "decency,"
"fine-looking," "dignity" or any of the other galaxies
of affirmative nouns and modifiers which are reserved
in these kinds of books for those of Anglo-Saxon
stock or those who are sufficiently close to Anglo-
Saxons to share a part of their white pride. At the
end of this section, the author suggests that it is the
presence of the white man within Africa which al-
lows some room for hope:

"Our airplane circles over the grasslands and then
flies back again down the Congo to the capital city
of Leopoldville. This town has many white people
living in it." The point of this, the intention, seems
to be that the reader will feel relieved. "Most are
from Belgium, the country of Europe that has made
the Congo Valley its colony. The Belgians govern the
Congo. They run the steamships and the railroads.
They have set out plantations of cotton, sugar cane,
peanuts, and cacao, and they direct the work of
gathering rubber from the wild Hevea trees . . .
They mine the copper in the mining districts and
they direct the trading stations . . . They believe

that they can develop the country better than the chiefs of the savage tribes, who know so little about modern ways."

In the same book there was also some strange writing about the Chinese. In this case it was not that we were told anything was wrong with looking odd or peculiar but simply that we were made to feel, beyond possibilities of redemption, that this "oddness," this "differentness," this "peculiarity" is something from which we can feel ourselves indescribably lucky to have been spared. It is the inexorable quality of differentness which seems so evil here. A bitter little perjury is perpetrated upon children even before they are old enough to understand exactly why it is that the things that are made to seem so different, strange and peculiar are precisely the things which it is easiest to despise. Of Chinese children: "They are different in appearance from any other children we have seen. Their skins are creamy yellow and their black eyes are set under narrow slanting lids. Their hair is black and coarse, and their cheek bones are high. They belong to the yellow race."

Looking at material like this, Americans may be forced to wonder what kind of country we were thirty years ago when this book was published. But then we also are forced to wonder whether we are really entirely changed today. For the alterations in many of the textbooks have not been enormous, and even in those where the apparent change has been considerable, the deeper change is slight. It may seem discouraging to add this but some of the worst among the newer books are worst precisely for the reason that they are trying so self-consciously and so pathetically to erase or to compensate for the prejudices of the earlier books. One of this kind, for example, used by one of the other Fourth Grade teachers at my school, was called *Journeys Through Many Lands*. In this book, as in the one discussed above, there was again no mention of any American Negroes but the authors at least made an heroic effort to overcome their repugnance to the African blacks. This, however, is what happens when people of good intention attempt to overcome a conditioned repugnance and to summon up complimentary words:

After they had given the Pygmies the same sort of drubbing that they get elsewhere, the authors of this book went on to admire the taller and, to them, more attractive Grassland Negroes. "These Negroes," said the authors, "are stronger and more intelligent than the Pygmies. They are fine, big black fel-

What kind of self-image will these children learn from their teachers? (Shelly Rusten)

lows . . ." After that, the authors went on to say
that these "fine, big black fellows" had plenty of
admirable qualities and for those qualities they were
then given unstinting praise. But the language that
had been used seemed to ruin everything afterward.
You could picture the British or American ambassa-
dor from a hundred years ago watching the Negroes
filing before him in the jungle and offering that
kind of cruel, misguided praise. But this is the question, disquieting or not, to which an answer must be
given: How long can the parents of any Negro child
in a nation which talks about democracy and fair
play be expected to stand by in passivity and pa-
tience while their child sweats out his lessons and
drains away his self-respect and dignity in the obedi-
ent study of such books as these? It does not even
matter if all of these books should be found out,
discovered, filtered off and taken away. The teachers
who believe in those books are still teaching and
until they stop teaching, or stop believing, the as-
sumptions will live on and the dignity of the children will decay.

What follows is a short story in which one of the characters expresses her views on race. As you read you will see that, compared to her Virginia-born husband, she regards herself as very liberal when it comes to this subject.

**13**

# Arrangement in Black and White

by DOROTHY PARKER

THE WOMAN with the pink velvet poppies twined round the assisted gold of her hair traversed the crowded room at an interesting gait combining a skip with a sidle, and clutched the lean arm of her host.

"Now I got you!" she said. "Now you can't get away!"

From *The Portable Dorothy Parker* (New York: The Viking Press, The Viking Portable Library, 1944), pp. 41–46. Copyright 1927, © 1955 by Dorothy Parker. Originally appeared in *The New Yorker*. Reprinted by permission of The Viking Press, Inc.

"Why, hello," said her host. "Well. How are you?"

"Oh, I'm finely," she said. "Just simply finely. Listen. I want you to do me the most terrible favor. Will you? Will you please? Pretty please?"

"What is it?" said her host.

"Listen," she said. "I want to meet Walter Williams. Honestly, I'm just simply crazy about that man. Oh, when he sings! When he sings those spirituals! Well, I said to Burton, 'It's a good thing for you Walter Williams is colored,' I said, 'or you'd have lots of reason to be jealous.' I'd really love to meet him. I'd like to tell him I've heard him sing. Will you be an angel and introduce me to him?"

"Why, certainly," said her host. "I thought you'd met him. The party's for him. Where is he, anyway?"

"He's over there by the bookcase," she said. "Let's wait till those people get through talking to him. Well, I think you're simply marvelous, giving this perfectly marvelous party for him, and having him meet all these white people, and all. Isn't he terribly grateful?"

"I hope not," said her host.

"I think it's really terribly nice," she said. "I do. I don't see why on earth it isn't perfectly all right to meet colored people. I haven't any feeling at all about it—not one single bit. Burton—oh, he's just the other way. Well, you know, he comes from Virginia, and you know how they are."

"Did he come tonight?" said her host.

"No, he couldn't," she said. "I'm a regular grass widow tonight. I told him when I left, 'There's no telling what I'll do,' I said. He was just so tired out, he couldn't move. Isn't it a shame?"

"Ah," said her host.

"Wait till I tell him I met Walter Williams!" she said. "He'll just about die. Oh, we have more argu-

ments about colored people. I talk to him like I
don't know what, I get so excited. 'Oh, don't be so
silly,' I say. But I must say for Burton, he's heaps
broader-minded than lots of these Southerners. He's
really awfully fond of colored people. Well, he says
himself, he wouldn't have white servants. And you
know, he had this old colored nurse, this regular old
nigger mammy, and he just simply loves her. Why,
every time he goes home, he goes out in the kitchen
to see her. He does, really, to this day. All he says
is, he says he hasn't got a word to say against colored people as long as they keep their place. He's
always doing things for them—giving them clothes
and I don't know what all. The only thing he says,
he says he wouldn't sit down at the table with one
for a million dollars. 'Oh,' I say to him, 'you make
me sick, talking like that.' I'm just terrible to him.
Aren't I terrible?"

"Oh, no, no, no," said her host. "No, no."

"I am," she said. "I know I am. Poor Burton!
Now, me, I don't feel that way at all. I haven't the
slightest feeling about colored people. Why, I'm just
crazy about some of them. They're just like children
—just as easygoing, and always singing and laughing and everything. Aren't they the happiest things
you ever saw in your life? Honestly, it makes me
laugh just to hear them. Oh, I like them. I really do.
Well, now, listen, I have this colored laundress, I've
had her for years, and I'm devoted to her. She's a
real character. And I want to tell you, I think of her
as my friend. That's the way I think of her. As I
say to Burton, 'Well, for heaven's sakes, we're all
human beings!' Aren't we?"

"Yes," said her host. "Yes, indeed."

"Now this Walter Williams," she said. "I think a
man like that's a real artist. I do. I think he de-

serves an awful lot of credit. Goodness, I'm so crazy about music or anything, I don't care *what* color he is. I honestly think if a person's an artist, nobody ought to have any feeling at all about meeting them. That's absolutely what I say to Burton. Don't you think I'm right?"

"Yes," said her host. "Oh, yes."

"That's the way I feel," she said. "I just can't understand people being narrow-minded. Why, I absolutely think it's a privilege to meet a man like Walter Williams. Yes, I do. I haven't any feeling at all. Well, my goodness, the good Lord made him, just the same as He did any of us. Didn't He?"

"Surely," said her host. "Yes, indeed."

"That's what I say," she said. "Oh, I get so furious when people are narrow-minded about colored people. It's just all I can do not to say something. Of course, I do admit when you get a bad colored man, they're simply terrible. But as I say to Burton, there are some bad white people, too, in this world. Aren't there?"

"I guess there are," said her host.

"Why, I'd really be glad to have a man like Walter Williams come to my house and sing for us, some time," she said. "Of course, I couldn't ask him on account of Burton, but I wouldn't have any feeling about it at all. Oh, can't he sing! Isn't it marvelous, the way they all have music in them? It just seems to be right *in* them. Come on, let's go on over and talk to him. Listen, what shall I do when I'm introduced? Ought I to shake hands? Or what?"

"Why, do whatever you want," said her host.

"I guess maybe I'd better," she said. "I wouldn't for the world have him think I had any feeling. I think I'd better shake hands, just the way I would with anybody else. That's just exactly what I'll do."

They reached the tall young Negro, standing by the bookcase. The host performed introductions; the Negro bowed.

"How do you do?" he said.

The woman with the pink velvet poppies extended her hand at the length of her arm and held it so for all the world to see, until the Negro took it, shook it, and gave it back to her.

"Oh, how do you do, Mr. Williams," she said. "Well, how do you do. I've just been saying, I've enjoyed your singing so awfully much. I've been to your concerts, and we have you on the phonograph and everything. Oh, I just enjoy it!"

She spoke with great distinctness, moving her lips meticulously, as if in parlance with the deaf.

"I'm so glad," he said.

"I'm just simply crazy about that 'Water Boy' thing you sing," she said. "Honestly, I can't get it out of my head. I have my husband nearly crazy, the way I go around humming it all the time. Oh, he looks just as black as the ace of—Well. Tell me, where on earth do you ever get all those songs of yours? How do you ever get hold of them?"

"Why," he said, "there are so many different——"

"I should think you'd love singing them," she said. "It must be more fun. All those darling old spirituals—oh, I just love them! Well, what are you doing, now? Are you still keeping up your singing? Why don't you have another concert, some time?"

"I'm having one the sixteenth of this month," he said.

"Well, I'll be there," she said. "I'll be there, if I possibly can. You can count on me. Goodness, here comes a whole raft of people to talk to you. You're just a regular guest of honor! Oh, who's that girl in white? I've seen her some place."

"That's Katherine Burke," said her host.

"Good Heavens," she said, "is that Katherine Burke? Why, she looks entirely different off the stage. I thought she was much better-looking. I had no idea she was so terribly dark. Why, she looks almost like—Oh, I think she's a wonderful actress! Don't you think she's a wonderful actress, Mr. Williams? Oh, I think she's marvelous. Don't you?"

"Yes, I do," he said.

Klan children learn early the hypocritical white attitudes of their parents. (UPI)

"Oh, I do, too," she said. "Just wonderful. Well, goodness, we must give someone else a chance to talk to the guest of honor. Now, don't forget, Mr. Williams, I'm going to be at that concert if I possibly can. I'll be there applauding like everything. And if I can't come, I'm going to tell everybody I know to go, anyway. Don't you forget!"

"I won't," he said. "Thank you so much."

The host took her arm and piloted her into the next room.

"Oh, my dear," she said. "I nearly died! Honestly, give you my word, I nearly passed away. Did you hear that terrible break I made? I was just going to say Katherine Burke looked almost like a nigger. I just caught myself in time. Oh, do you think he noticed?"

"I don't believe so," said her host.

"Well, thank goodness," she said, "because I wouldn't have embarrassed him for anything. Why, he's awfully nice. Just as nice as he can be. Nice manners, and everything. You know, so many colored people, you give them an inch, and they walk all over you. But he doesn't try any of that. Well, he's got more sense, I suppose. He's really nice. Don't you think so?"

"Yes," said her host.

"I liked him," she said. "I haven't any feeling at all because he's a colored man. I felt just as natural as I would with anybody. Talked to him just as naturally, and everything. But honestly, I could hardly keep a straight face. I kept thinking of Burton. Oh, wait till I tell Burton I called him 'Mister'!"

In this selection a former Imperial Wizard of the Ku Klux Klan explains his stand and that of the organization which he led on matters of race and on the reasons he felt that the Klan was performing a useful function in American society.

# 14

## The Klan's Fight for Americanism

by HIRA W. EVANS

THE KLAN, therefore, has now come to speak for the great mass of Americans of the old pioneer stock. We believe that it does fairly and faithfully represent them, and our proof lies in their support. To understand the Klan, then, it is necessary to understand the character and present mind of the mass of old-stock Americans. The mass, it must be remembered, as distinguished from the intellectually mongrelized "Liberals."

These are, in the first place, a blend of various peoples of the so-called Nordic race, the race which,

From *Great Issues in American History*, Vol. 2: 1864–1954 edited by Richard Hofstadter (New York: Vintage Books, Alfred A. Knopf, Inc., 1958), pp. 325–31.

Robert M. Shelton, the Imperial Wizard of the Klan, recruits members in Dearborn, Michigan (February 1970). (UPI)

with all its faults, has given the world almost the whole of modern civilization. The Klan does not try to represent any people but these.

There is no need to recount the virtues of the American pioneers; but it is too often forgotten that in the pioneer period a selective process of intense rigor went on. From the first only hardy, adventurous and strong men and women dared the pioneer dangers; from among these all but the best died swiftly, so that the new Nordic blend which became the American race was bred up to a point probably the highest in history. This remarkable race character, along with the new-won continent and the new-created nation, made the inheritance of the old-stock Americans the richest ever given to a generation of men.

In spite of it, however, these Nordic Americans for the last generation have found themselves increasingly uncomfortable, and finally deeply distressed. There appeared first confusion in thought and opinion, a groping and hesitancy about national affairs and private life alike, in sharp contrast to the clear, straightforward purposes of our earlier years. There was futility in religion, too, which was in many ways even more distressing. Presently we began to find that we were dealing with strange ideas; policies that always sounded well, but somehow always made us still more uncomfortable.

Finally came the moral breakdown that has been going on for two decades. One by one all our traditional moral standards went by the boards, or were so disregarded that they ceased to be binding. The sacredness of our Sabbath, of our homes, of chastity, and finally even of our right to teach our own children in our own schools fundamental facts and truths were torn away from us. Those who maintained the old standards did so only in the face of constant ridicule.

Along with this went economic distress. The assurance for the future of our children dwindled. We found our great cities and the control of much of our industry and commerce taken over by strangers, who stacked the cards of success and prosperity against us. Shortly they came to dominate our government. The *bloc* system by which this was done is now familiar to all. Every kind of inhabitant except the Americans gathered in groups which operated as units in politics, under orders of corrupt, self-seeking and un-American leaders, who both by purchase and threat enforced their demands on politicians. Thus it came about that the interests of Americans were always the last to be considered by either national or city governments, and that the native Americans were constantly discriminated against, in business, in legislation and in administrative government.

So the Nordic American today is a stranger in large parts of the land his fathers gave him. Moreover, he is a most unwelcome stranger, one much spit upon, and one to whom even the right to have his own opinions and to work for his own interests is now denied with jeers and revilings. "We must Americanize the Americans," a distinguished immigrant said recently. Can anything more clearly show the state to which the real American has fallen in this country which was once his own?

Our falling birth rate, the result of all this, is proof of our distress. We no longer feel that we can be fair to children we bring into the world, unless we can make sure from the start that they shall have capital or education or both, so that they need never compete with those who now fill the lower rungs of the ladder of success. We dare no longer risk letting our youth "make its own way" in the conditions under which we live. So even our unborn children are being crowded out of their birthright!

All this has been true for years, but it was the World War that gave us our first hint of the real cause of our troubles, and began to crystallize our ideas. The war revealed that millions whom we had allowed to share our heritage and prosperity, and whom we had assumed had become part of us, were in fact not wholly so. They had other loyalties: each was willing—anxious!—to sacrifice the interests of the country that had given him shelter to the interests of the one he was supposed to have cast off; each in fact did use the freedom and political power we had given him against ourselves whenever he could see any profit for his older loyalty.

This, of course, was chiefly in international affairs, and the excitement caused by the discovery of disloyalty subsided rapidly after the war ended. But it was not forgotten by the Nordic Americans. They had been awakened and alarmed; they began to suspect that the hyphenism which had been shown was only a part of what existed; their quiet was not that of renewed sleep, but of strong men waiting very watchfully. And presently they began to form decisions about all those aliens who were Americans for profit only.

They decided that even the crossing of salt-water did not dim a single spot on a leopard; that an alien usually remains an alien no matter what is done to him, what veneer of education he gets, what oaths he takes, nor what public attitudes he adopts. They decided that the melting pot was a ghastly failure, and remembered that the very name was coined by a member of one of the races—the Jews—

which most determinedly refuses to melt. They decided that in every way, as well as in politics, the alien in the vast majority of cases is unalterably fixed in his instincts, character, thought and interests by centuries of racial selection and development, that he thinks first for his own people, works only with and for them, cares entirely for their interests, considers himself always one of them, and never an American. They decided that in character, instincts, thought, and purposes—in his whole soul—an alien remains fixedly alien to America and all it means.

They saw, too, that the alien was tearing down the American standard of living, especially in the lower walks. It became clear that while the American can out-work the alien, the alien can so far under-live the American as to force him out of all competitive labor. So they came to realize that the Nordic can easily survive and rule and increase if he holds for himself the advantages won by strength and daring of his ancestors in times of stress and peril, but that if he surrenders those advantages to the peoples who could not share the stress, he will soon be driven below the level at which he can exist by their low standards, low living and fast breeding. And they saw that the low standard aliens of Eastern and Southern Europe were doing just that thing to us.

They learned, though more slowly, that alien ideas are just as dangerous to us as the aliens themselves, no matter how plausible such ideas may sound. With most of the plain people this conclusion is based simply on the fact that the alien ideas do not work well for them. Others went deeper and came to understand that the differences in racial background, in breeding, instinct, character and emotional point of view are more important than logic. So ideas which may be perfectly healthy for an alien may also be poisonous for Americans.

Finally they learned the great secret of the propagandists; that success in corrupting public opinion depends on putting out the subversive ideas without revealing their source. They came to suspect that "prejudice" against foreign ideas is really a protective device of nature against mental food that may be indigestible. They saw, finally, that the alien leaders in America act on this theory, and that there is a steady flood of alien ideas being spread over the country, always carefully disguised as American.

As they learned all this the Nordic Americans have been gradually arousing themselves to defend their homes and their own kind of civilization. They have not known just how to go about it; the idealist philanthropy and good-natured generosity which led to the philosophy of the melting pot have died hard. Resistance to the peaceful invasion of the immigrant is no such simple matter as snatching up weapons and defending frontiers, nor has it much spectacular emotionalism to draw men to the colors.

The old-stock Americans are learning, however. They have begun to arm themselves for this new type of warfare. Most important, they have broken away from the fetters of the false ideals and philanthropy which put aliens ahead of their own children and their own race.

To do this they have had to reject completely— and perhaps for the moment the rejection is a bit too complete—the whole body of "Liberal" ideas which they had followed with such simple, unquestioning faith. The first and immediate cause of the break with Liberalism was that it had provided no defense against the alien invasion, but instead had excused it—even defended it against Americanism.

Liberalism is today charged in the mind of most Americans with nothing less than national, racial and spiritual treason. . . .

We are a movement of the plain people, very weak in the matter of culture, intellectual support, and trained leadership. We are demanding, and we expect to win, a return of power into the hands of the everyday, not highly cultured, not overly intellectualized, but entirely unspoiled and not de-Americanized, average citizen of the old stock. Our members and leaders are all of this class—the opposition of the intellectuals and liberals who held the leadership, betrayed Americanism, and from whom we expect to wrest control, is almost automatic.

This is undoubtedly a weakness. It lays us open to the charge of being "hicks" and "rubes" and "drivers of secondhand Fords." We admit it. Far worse, it makes it hard for us to state our case and advocate our crusade in the most effective way, for most of us lack skill in language. Worst of all, the need of trained leaders constantly hampers our progress and leads to serious blunders and internal troubles. If the Klan ever should fail it would be from this cause. All this we on the inside know far better than our critics, and regret more. Our leadership is improving, but for many years the Klan will be seeking better leaders, and the leaders praying for greater wisdom.

Serious as this is, and strange though our attitude may seem to the intellectuals, it does not worry us greatly. Every popular movement has suffered from just this handicap, yet the popular movements have been the mainsprings of progress, and have usually had to win against the "best people" of their time. Moreover, we can depend on getting this intellectual backing shortly. It is notable that when the plain people begin to win with one of their movements, such as the Klan, the very intellectuals who have scoffed and fought most bitterly presently begin to dig up sound—at least well-sounding!—logic in support of the success. The movement, so far as can be judged, is neither hurt nor helped by this process. . . .

Our critics have accused us of being merely a "protest movement," of being frightened; they say we fear alien competition, are in a panic because we cannot hold our own against the foreigners. That is partly true. We are a protest movement—protesting against being robbed. We are afraid of competition with peoples who would destroy our standard of living. We are suffering in many ways, we have been betrayed by our trusted leaders, we are half beaten already. But we are not frightened nor in a panic. We have merely awakened to the fact that we must fight for our own. We are going to fight—and win!

The Klan does not believe that the fact that it is emotional and instinctive, rather than coldly intellectual, is a weakness. All action comes from emotion, rather than from ratiocination. Our emotions and the instincts on which they are based have been bred into us for thousands of years; far longer than reason has had a place in the human brain. They are the many-times distilled products of experience; they still operate much more surely and promptly than reason can. For centuries those who obeyed them have lived and carried on the race; those in whom they were weak, or who failed to obey, have died. They are the foundations of our American civilization, even more than our great historic documents; they can be trusted where the fine-haired reasoning of the denatured intellectuals cannot. . . .

Poetry is one of the rhythmic ways that man can express his despair, his desires, his dreams, in order to better understand himself and the society in which he lives. The three poems below are voices crying out against racial injustice.

**15**

# Dream Variation

by LANGSTON HUGHES

To fling my arms wide
In some place of the sun,
To whirl and to dance
Till the white day is done.
Then rest at cool evening
Beneath a tall tree
While night comes on gently,
     Dark like me—
That is my dream!

To fling my arms wide
In the face of the sun,
Dance! Whirl! Whirl!
Till the quick day is done.
Rest at pale evening . . .
A tall, slim tree . . .
Night coming tenderly
　　Black like me.

"To whirl and to dance
　Till the white day is done."　(Ed Lettau)

In the midst of a bitter integration fight in their community, black and white boys play together. (Wide World)

# Tableau

by COUNTEE CULLEN

*For Donald Duff*

Locked arm in arm they cross the way,
   The black boy and the white,
The golden splendor of the day,
   The sable pride of night.

From lowered blinds the dark folk stare,
   And here the fair folk talk,
Indignant that these two should dare
   In unison to walk.

Oblivious to look and word
   They pass, and see no wonder
That lightning brilliant as a sword
   Should blaze the path of thunder.

Descendants of the people of the Ghost Dance religion, Dakota Sioux Indians perform the Sun Dance. (Richard Erdoes)

# A Sequence of Songs of the Ghost Dance Religion

by PLAINS INDIANS

### 1.

My children,
When at first I liked the whites,
I gave them fruits,
I gave them fruits.

### 2.

Father have pity on me,
I am crying for thirst,
All is gone,
I have nothing to eat.

### 3.

The father will descend,
The earth will tremble,
Everybody will arise,
Stretch out your hands.

*A Sequence of Songs of the Ghost Dance Religion*, by Plains Indians, was originally published in an article "The Ghost Dance Religion and the Sioux Outbreak of 1890" by James Mooney which was part of the 14th Annual Report of the Bureau of American Ethnology, Washington, 1896.

### 4.

The Crow—*Ehe′eye!*
I saw him when he flew down,
To the earth, to the earth.
He has renewed our life,
He has taken pity on us.

### 5.

I circle around
The boundaries of the earth,
Wearing the long wing feathers,
As I fly.

### 6.

I′yehé! my children—
My children,
We have rendered them desolate.
The whites are crazy—Ahe′yuhe′yu!

### 7.

We shall live again,
We shall live again.

**Notes**

**Index**

# Notes

1. Ashley Montagu, *What We Know About Race* (New York: The One Nation Library, Anti-Defamation League of B'nai B'rith, 1968), p. 4.
2. *Ibid,* p. 10.
3. Hermann Rauschning, *The Voice of Destruction* (New York: G. P. Putnam's Sons, 1940), p. 232.
4. *The Crisis,* XVIII May, 1919, pp. 16–17.
5. U.S. Commission on Civil Rights, *Racial Isolation in the Public School* (Washington, D.C.: Government Printing Office, 1967), p. 1.
6. National Education Association, Conference on the Treatment of Minorities in Textbooks and Other Reading Materials, Washington, D. C., 1967.
7. Charles Y. Glock and Ellen Siegelman, editors, *Prejudice, U.S.A.* (New York: Praeger, 1969), pp. 185–86.
8. John Herbers, "Discrimination Held Main Cause of Income Inequality," *The New York Times,* February 25, 1970, p. 18.
9. *Chicago Daily News,* September 11, 1967.

10. Bayard Rustin, "The Anatomy of Frustration," an address delivered at the 55th National Commission Meeting of the Anti-Defamation League of B'nai B'rith, May 6, 1968, New York, N. Y.

11. Lucy S. Davidowicz, *Negro and Jew, An Encounter in America.* Shlomo Katz, editor. (Toronto, Ontario: The Macmillan Company, 1969), p. 18.

12. "Excerpts from Ribicoff Rights Speech," *The New York Times,* February 10, 1970, p. 29.

# Index

**189**

## GENERAL EDITOR

Gerald Leinwand is Professor of Education and Chairman of the Department of Education at the Bernard M. Baruch College of the City University of New York. Dr. Leinwand received his B.A., M.S., and Ph.D. degrees from New York University and an M.A. from Columbia University. In addition to numerous magazine articles, he is the author of *The Pageant of World History, The American Constitution: A Tutor-Text,* and a college text *Teaching History and the Social Studies in Secondary Schools.*